4/01

Performing the Force

D0851776

For Brooks

Performing the Force

Essays on Immersion into Science Fiction, Fantasy and Horror Environments

Edited by Kurt Lancaster *and* Tom Mikotowicz

McFarland & Company, Inc., Publishers
Jefferson, North Carolina, and London

Library of Congress Cataloguing-in-Publication Data

Performing the force : essays on immersion into science
fiction, fantasy and horror environments / edited by
Kurt Lancaster and Tom Mikotowicz.
　　　　p.　　cm.
　　Includes bibliographical references and index.
　　ISBN 0-7864-0895-2 (softcover : 50# alkaline paper) ∞
　　1. Interactive multimedia.　　2. Virtual reality.
　I. Lancaster, Kurt, 1967–　　II. Mikotowicz, Thomas J.
　QA76.76.I59P47　　2001
　006.7 — dc21　　　　　　　　　　　　　　　　00-067652

British Library cataloguing data are available

Cover Image ©2001 Wood River Gallery

Manufactured in the United States of America

McFarland & Company, Inc., Publishers
　Box 611, Jefferson, North Carolina 28640
　　www.mcfarlandpub.com

Contents

Part III
Performing in Computer Games

Part IV
At the Interface: Webpages as Sites of Immersion

Part V
Interactive Movies

Part VI
Marketing and Playing with Action Figures

Part VII
Performing in Role-Playing Games

Part VIII
Environmental Fantasies

Acknowledgments

I would like to thank Una Chaudhuri, who gave me the opportunity to teach my first class in the Department of Drama at NYU's Tisch School of the Arts. I also want to thank each and every one of my students at NYU for giving me a superb first teaching experience.

Kurt Lancaster

Special thanks go to the University of Maine for its support for this project.

Tom Mikotowicz

Introduction: Popular Entertainment and the Desire for Transcendence: Immersion into Science Fiction, Fantasy, and Horror Performances

BY KURT LANCASTER AND TOM MIKOTOWICZ

People in the Western world have had of late a growing desire to deeply immerse themselves into the performance of science fiction, fantasy, and horror. The characters, images, and language from such varied entertainments as *Star Wars*, *Star Trek*, *The Lord of the Rings*, and *The X-Files* have spawned such participatory media as role-playing and computer games, websites, and artificial entertainment environments, as well as found their way into everyday life. This emerging cultural phenomenon, which has been fed by new technologies such as the internet and computer gaming as well as the commercial process of marketing entertainments, may stem from the need for fans to transcend their mundane everyday lives and experience firsthand the fantasies with which they are intimately familiar through movies, television, books, and games. This collection of essays—which grew out of a performance studies course Kurt taught at NYU in Fall 1998—provides a description of these various sites. It analyzes the performative elements of the fan's immersion into the material culture of fantasy environments.

The authors are not scholars but are themselves fans who have explored firsthand what it means to become immersed into new sites of performance. These author/fans describe how the work of their favorite creators

1

of science fiction, fantasy, and horror—whether filmmakers, novelists, or game creators—becomes circulated through popular culture and reveals the hidden codes and values of that culture. They show that through touching, playing, and performing with the cultural artifacts of science fiction, fantasy, and horror, people become immersed in sites of performance; further, they examine why people desire to visit such places. Beneath the surface performance, suggest the authors, is a deeper desire for the transcendent—fans' heartfelt examination of the limits of everyday life and the need to enter otherworldly environments in order to become more than they are. Because each site is different, participants experience various fantasy universes from different perspectives. For example, fans can perform a vampire in a role-playing game, cast spells in a fantasy game, design a web page as an homage to their favorite director, play with action figures based on popular television shows and films, and even portray a powerful warrior in a computer war game.

People in conventional entertainment forms participate vicariously through another's performance, but they cannot control the plot or the dramatic action. The performances comprising the sites described in this book, on the other hand, require a different kind of participatory technique: participants have to actively engage the site as performers. Formerly, such fantasies as Straczynski's *Babylon 5*, Lucas's *Star Wars*, Roddenberry's *Star Trek*, and Tolkien's *Middle-earth*, to name a few, could only be experienced through the scopic forms of cinema, television, and novels (through the theater of the mind). Now, however, people can also experience imaginary environments through the pores of other senses: environments that encompass sight, sound, and touch. Whether it is in the role-playing game, a war game, a computer game, or a web design, the centrality of linear narratives has been replaced by immersive and interactive participation in the imaginary environments of science fiction, fantasy, and horror.

Exploring the cultural significance of imaginary entertainment environments, the authors provide a description of each site, analyzing each one as a kind of performance. They are not critics, nor are they cultural scholars; rather, the authors are describing their personal experiences as immersive participants into various sites of fantasy, sites that they, perhaps, have been enamored with since childhood. Since they are speaking from personal experience, this book is not an exhaustive study, but is limited to the authors' personal perspectives as fans. These author/fans, however, have been exposed to the scholarly ideas formulated by such performance theorists as Richard Schechner and Jon McKenzie, sociologist Erving Goffman, and linguistic philosophers J. L. Austin and Roland

Barthes. They use these theories as a way to help explain how these fantasy sites work and, at the same time, what this means in a broader cultural context.

Performance theory (or performance studies) had its beginnings in the 1960s theatrical avant-garde. Discontented with conventional European and American drama and proscenium stages where spectators are cut off from the spectators, the avant-garde incorporated the traditional performances and performance training from indigenous cultures around the world while, in some instances, encompassing the spectators into their performances. Realizing that the conventional institutions of theater in higher education were still stuck with examining conventional plays and productions— including the training of students in such schools (who are still trained to believe that there are enough jobs in the theater to keep pumping out such starry-eyed students)— the Department of Graduate Drama at New York University's Tisch School of the Arts said no to this approach by the early 1970s. Renaming themselves the Department of Performance Studies in 1980, the professors at this university trained students in intercultural performance forms and unconventional production techniques— the stuff of the avant-garde — and, most importantly, gave them the tools to examine all performance forms, whether those performances occur on a conventional stage, in cyberspace, or in wider popular culture forms. Some of their scholarly approaches are used in this book.

Performance theory, as espoused by Richard Schechner, presents two important theories positing how performance is enacted. First, "strips" of living behavior may be "treated as a film director treats a strip of film" (1985:35). "The performers get in touch with, recover, remember, or even invent these strips of behavior," Schechner contends, "and then rebehave according to these strips, either by being absorbed into them (playing a role, going into trance) or by existing side by side with them (Brecht's *Verfremdungseffekt*)" (36). In the various sites of science fiction, fantasy, and horror, various strips of behavior originating in the initial site (such as a novel, film, or television show) become embedded into such participatory sites as web pages, role-playing games, war games, computer games, Disney theme park rides, and so on.

In his second theory, Schechner distinguishes four concentric layers occurring during a performance: the frames of drama, script, theater, and performance (1988:72). The drama represents the innermost frame. It is what the writer writes—composed of a "written text, score, scenario, instruction, plan, or map." It is "intense (heated up)." This frame lies within the "domain of the author," and it is detached from the actual "doing" of the text or scenario. In the case of science-fiction, fantasy, and horror environments, the drama is found in the originating text, whether that is in Lucas's *Star Wars* or in Tolkien's *The Lord of the Rings*.

The script is the performance text — all of the elements going into the interpretation and enactment of the drama. The script is "the basic code of events" or "patterns of doing" (70) inscribed into the performers' bodies as modes of behavior. It guides the performers in letting them know what to do and how to do it. The script is the interior map of the production that occurs in the theatrical frame. The script lies in the domain of the teacher, master, or director. In the case of web pages, fantasy games, and other sites of performance the script may comprise the rules of the games, the tools in creating the website, and all of the physical elements that allow participants to immerse themselves into fantasy. It is everything that allows fans to participate in certain ways, whether one is using a joystick to fly an X-Wing fighter in a computer game or to move a miniature orc in the war game *Warhammer*.

The theater frame is the "manifestation or representation of the drama and/or script." It is what visibly occurs onstage — whether that is the exterior map board of a war game, a visual interface on a computer screen, or the examination of a "ghost-town" in an ambulatory walk through the woods. It is the mise-en-scène through which the participants become immersed. The outermost, performance frame represents the "whole constellation of events, most of them passing unnoticed, that take place in and among both performers and audience" (72). This is what the spectators see onstage and in the auditorium, and in most conventional play productions it is a direct manifestation of what is written down in the play and viewed by sitting spectators. In participatory science-fiction, fantasy, and horror environments, it is everything that occurs before, during, and after immersion. For example, the performance of *Star Wars* does not begin and end in a movie house. The corporate advertising of *Star Wars* toys, the display of the toys in a store, and the purchase of an action figure by a fan who opens up the package and plays with it all become a part of the performance of *Star Wars* under this definition.

The corporate performance form (as seen in *Star Wars* merchandising) is the concern of theorist Jon McKenzie, who examines the performance of corporate advertising and how it manipulates the consumer. "Bureaucratic performance is the language game of big money, and it is run by the numerical values of profitability, cost-effectiveness, and optimization" (1997:47). McKenzie takes Schechner's theory of restored behaviors and applies it as a cultural trope through which commodity is circulated: an "embodiment of social archives, the restoration and transformation of historical forces in living behavior" (31). Science-fiction, fantasy, and horror environments are the very embodiment of archived film, television, and novels becoming transformed by fans into the living behavior of their participatory performances, whether that occurs with an action figure or in a computer game.

Also important to the approach of these authors are the theories of Erving Goffman, who theorized the "presentation of self in everyday life" 40 years ago. Goffman states that this presentational behavior comprises "all the activity of a given participant on a given occasion which serves to influence in any way any of the other participants" (1959:15). In essence, a person performing in this mode attempts to "control the conduct of others, especially their responsive treatment of him" (3). Goffman believes that people project a social front — what one could call a personality type — in much the same way as an actor performs a role. In the case of science-fiction, fantasy, and horror environments, however, fans are assuming fictional roles (as presented in novels, television, and films) and re-presenting those in everyday life. Whether they equip themselves with a Darth Maul lightsaber or say, "May the Force be with you," they are attempting to share with others their sense of wonder that they have received from the viewing of a film by re-performing the transcendent belief that they received when first exposed to the otherworldly environment onscreen.

The authors examine verbal performances through the ideas of J. L. Austin, who theorized that when people state certain speech acts they are not just describing an event, but actually performing it. A "performative utterance," Austin explains, is used in "performing an action" (1975 [1962]:6). The verbalization of a statement (such as "I do" at a wedding ceremony; or when "I," a character, "pull out my battle-axe" in a role-playing game) comprises the action of what is done. A performative "is not to describe my doing ... it is to do it," Austin contends (6). In a role-playing game performance, for example, players do not just improvisationally describe what their characters will do in a given scene: what they say is the action itself, and that very act induces the performers and audience into a new context — activating an imaginary fantasy environment.

Furthermore, this activation and immersion into science fiction, fantasy, and horror is a linguistic outcome, as Roland Barthes would contend. There are inherent patterns of thought or meaning — what he terms social and cultural codes — placed within various images and texts that manipulate people into accepting a fantasy as a reality. Barthes believes that knowledge is passed down through the ages in such a way that we assume this knowledge and the desire for this knowledge is natural. He contends, however, that the "meaning" of a "signifier" is not inherent in its form, but a discrete identity that becomes distorted when a meaning is imposed on the form linguistically (1972 [1957]:128). This distortion, in which an idea is used to manipulate an image, constitutes what Barthes calls mythology: "everything happens as if the picture *naturally* conjured up the concept, as if the signifier [the image] *gave a foundation* to the signified [the concept]" (129–130). In Barthes's definition of mythology, the concept becomes the dominant ideology, which is born when specific ideas are used to manipulate images. Barthes might say that the need for the performance of science fiction, fantasy, and horror is nothing more than a linguistic code so deeply embedded in our society that we see it as being a natural desire, while in fact it is only a manipulation of a cultural code: "the code of knowledge, or rather of human knowledge, public opinion, of culture as transmitted through books, education, and in a more general, more diffuse way, through all sociality; a body of rules so widely used that we take them as natural features" (1985:94).

Sites of performance are never natural, but the desire to become immersed within them becomes *as if* natural. What remains clear is that people, whether conscious of manipulative cultural codes or not, desire this immersion as they have always desired it even before science fiction, fantasy, and horror became popular terms of the twentieth century. Why? Because, as Joseph Roach, contends, every time a vacancy occurs within culture, a surrogate is created to fill in the remaining vacuum of desire, "as actual or perceived vacancies occur in the network of relations that constitutes the social fabric. Into the cavities created by loss through death or *other forms of departures*, I hypothesize, survivors attempt to fit satisfactory alternatives" (1996:2; emphasis added). All of these various sites of performance are an attempt to find satisfaction in a life that is lacking fulfillment. Thus, in our postmodern world, people desire to turn to the fantastic, which is ultimately a turn to the transcendent.

PART I

The Desire for the Fantastic: Escape or Self-Elucidation?

The Quest: Dreams and Desires in Fantasy and Science Fiction

BY HEATHER JEAN FITCH

> *That I might drink, and leave the world unseen,*
> *And with thee fade away into the forest dim.*
>
> — John Keats

> *The images of myth are reflections of the spiritual potentialities*
> *of every one of us. Through contemplating these, we evoke their*
> *powers in our own lives.*
>
> — Joseph Campbell

> *These myths speak to me because they express what I know inside*
> *is true.*
>
> — Bill Moyers

I was about 15 the summer I went on my first canoe trip. One evening we were all sitting around the picnic table watching the electric lantern collect moths and one of the guys suggested we play *Dungeons & Dragons.* I had no idea what it really was; all I knew was that it was somehow associated with some people killing themselves* and had something to do with fantasy, which I loved. And besides, I had a crush on the guy who suggested it. We had none of the equipment necessary, except for a pair of dice, but Nate said that we could make up our own characters however

---

*The National Coalition on Television Violence linked *Dungeons & Dragons*—seemingly at the height of its popularity—to 29 murders and suicides occurring between 1979 and 1985. Private investigator William Dear, in *The Dungeon Master,* attributed 14-year-old prodigy Dallas Egbert's suicide to *D&D.* (For a more detailed history of these cases see Lancaster 1994.)

we wanted and he would be the gamemaster (the one in charge of the game's narrative). We played every evening for the rest of the trip. I was enthralled with the character that I had created, and I drew a detailed picture of her on the back of a paper bag. I was drawn very quickly into the fantasy journey that Nate led us on, and began to feel a desire, perhaps more of a need, for the world and story that we were creating. I began to feel the same way that I do when I read a really good fantasy novel — that the everyday world isn't enough, there must be something more. Only, it was more intense, because, as a participant, I was creating and sharing in the world of imagination.

Fantasy and science-fiction author and essayist Ursula K. Le Guin writes: "fantasy is the natural, the appropriate language for the recounting of the spiritual journey and the struggle of good and evil in the soul" (1979:64). Thus, we desire a knowledge that can come only from the struggles we encounter, the base of humanity, and it is science fiction and fantasy that allow us to face these challenges in order to learn. Moreover, through visions and images offered to us by these mythic forms, we are given a chance to encounter and accept the parts of ourselves that dwell in shadow. That is, we know there are no real dragons to fight, but is it the fight with the dragon that we truly desire, or the glory, revelation, and knowledge that come from that fight? Finally, these stories that we reenact over and over with the dragons and the wizards, the talking beasts, as well as with the aliens and space explorers, all come to us from the old myths, from symbols that have spanned the centuries, telling generation after generation about themselves, the gods, and the world. We perform these stories today, however, through novels, stories, and films, as well as through the role-playing culture of science fiction and fantasy.

To perform these stories is to begin to understand the hero's journey. It satisfies a certain need we carry within us: the need to understand the self as a hero and the journey that lies within all of us. By understanding that need, we can learn to come to terms with and understand ourselves, but where does this need spring from? In Roland Barthes's essay "Textual Analysis of a Tale of Poe," he discusses forms of textual analysis and what kinds of impact certain "codes" have within a text. Barthes would say that this need for performance of science fiction and fantasy is nothing more than a linguistic code so deeply embedded in our society that we see it as being a natural desire, while in fact it is only a manipulation of a cultural code: "the code of knowledge, or rather of human knowledge, public opinion, of culture as transmitted through books, education, and in a more general, more diffuse way, through all sociality ... a body of rules so widely used that we take them as natural features" (1985:94). Barthes argues that those things we take for granted within our knowledge of the world are not natural knowledge, but rather knowledge learned as a result of culture. In other words, the cultural code is knowledge we believe to be natural and innate, but is, in fact, taught to us by the culture we live in. It is taught in such a deep way that it is ingrained in us as if it were natural. Thus, re-performing this hero's journey, the strength of desire that we feel for this kind of knowledge is a desire that springs essentially from a body of societal rules that we accept as coming naturally to us because they are so ingrained.

There is, I believe, a deeper level than this. I am inclined to disagree with Barthes on that level. He is correct on the surface. For example, the dragon in the fantasy that I am reading is not necessarily a natural image, but one that has come to represent the evil creature that must be overcome. Thus the images are possibly learned, but perhaps the journey is not. Maybe there is an innate desire in humanity to follow the path of the hero that is not learned, a desire of the soul to know itself that is part of what makes us human.

In a series of interviews done by Bill Moyers with Joseph Campbell in *The Power of Myth* (1991 [1988]), Campbell shares his extensive knowledge about myth: "I think what we are looking for is a way of experiencing the world that will open to us the transcendent that informs it, and at the same time forms ourselves within it. That is what people want. That is what the soul asks for" (61). The soul asks for this journey because it is a longing embedded deeply within us. It has become defined by social and cultural codes through images created by language because that is the only way we can share this longing with each other. But at the root of these images, these stories, and these games is a need that is innate. It is our birthright as part of humanity to need what these myths satisfy.

In what other ways might this presentation of a mythic world be viewed? Fantasy and science-fiction fans find ways to play out their desire in the role-playing game, but it is also played out in day-to-day life with those who dress according to styles in fantasy (such as the dark-clothed Goth look) and use lingo that has been invented by fantasy. This kind of performance could be called a "social front," a phrase Erving Goffman uses in *The Presentation of Self in Everyday Life* (1959). A social front can be described as the mask under which we present ourselves to society. Through certain techniques, we see to it that the world views us in a particular way.

In many ways, the reenactment of science fiction and fantasy in today's culture is a social front. In the role-playing game, people take on the social fronts of the characters to present to the other players. If somebody is a real fantasy buff (and proud to be one), he or she will take on that front in everyday life as well. Again, I think we can take this further. Fantasy and science fiction are in themselves a social front. They present a face to society. It is the face of dragons, fairies, elves, starships, and hobbits; and it is the language of *thee* and *thou* and the magic, the knowledge and the power of the fantasy world. Underneath this social front lie humanity's deepest desires, for knowledge of the self and of the world. Myth is the social front for the hero's journey within every human soul. As humans, our powers are limited and our desires run deep, but we struggle with them, not understanding how they relate to us. So, we find ways to perform what we feel can answer those desires. Further, it must continue to be performed because our desires do not ever subside.

There are pieces of performance that Richard Schechner calls "restored behavior" (1985:35). "Strips" of behavior from the past are reenacted in plays or other performances. (The cultural codes of Barthes are often enacted in these strips of behavior.) Schechner describes this in terms of the rehearsal process. It can also be seen in this passing down of myth. Whenever a role-player creates a character, an author writes a fantasy or science-fiction novel, or a film incorporates the fantastic, strips of myth are produced. Those strips of myth restore the behavior of those who listened around campfires or stood in temples, telling the story of their lives and the lives of the gods, over and over, down through the ages.

In his book *Performance Theory* (1988), Schechner discusses the place of ritual in performance, contending that play derives from life situations, and indeed becomes a ritualization of such behavior (97). This "ritualized behavior" is a way to test the boundaries between play and "for real" (100). In our desire to have these worlds be "for real," we test our boundaries by means of reading stories, seeing films, engaging in gaming, and using our imaginations. We find that the borders between the imaginary and the real are perhaps not so clear as we thought, and that there is a liminal place in the middle where they mingle.

In Ursula K. Le Guin's fantasy novel *A Wizard of Earthsea* (1968), she tells the rather unusual story of a wizard who lets loose a demon to prove that he is powerful. He is, however, not trained enough to send it back once he has called it up, and the only way he can defeat it is to discover its true name. It chases him until about halfway though the book, at which point, exhausted, he turns and chases it over land and sea. Far out at the edge of the world, he finally defeats it by naming it with his own name. It is a part of him, and it held power over him only because he would not admit that he had a "shadow self."

This story is more of a typical myth than a standard fantasy novel because its meanings are not so much implied as they are straightforward. The meaning of this story is apparent in many fantasy tales, and as a result, Le Guin has, perhaps unwittingly, restored the behavior of a fantasy novel, and destroyed its social front. The cultural codes of fantasy are there (the wizards, the demons, the dragons), but she has laid bare what her story is *really* about, what all fantasy and science fiction is about. It is the age-old search for the self, in which we learn to accept aspects of the self that were previously denied or simply blocked out, in which we come to knowledge of the world through knowledge of our soul. "For example, a constant image is that of the eagle and the serpent. The serpent is bound to the earth, the eagle in spiritual flight — isn't that something we all experience? And then, when the two amalgamate, we get a wonderful dragon, a serpent with wings" (Campbell 1991:45). We see the eagle and the serpent, and we all want to be the eagle, denying our dark side. It is only in the willingness to accept our humanity and combine the two sides, however, that we get the majesty of the dragon. "Heaven and hell are within us," Campbell contends "and all the gods are within us" (46).

In fantasy thinking, "I am not enough as I am," hence there is a desire to create a fantasy character in whom "I am more." In role-playing, we restore the behavior of the characters we have read about, bringing them to life again and again. In my earlier *Dungeons & Dragons* game, I laughed out loud as I gave my character a face of strength, power, and beauty because she was everything that I wanted. Filled with power and excitement, I stepped into the world of my dreams, my cloak blowing about me in the wind. People who say they have never felt that deep desire to "leave the world unseen," and never longed to take the magic step that leads into the world of dreams, may not be admitting their humanity. Many of us pretend that it is a desire that passes when our books of "make-believe" are put aside, when costume boxes and dreams are given away. If you believe that, you are fooling yourself. A dream is not so easy to get rid of. If it is dismissed, its shadow will dwell in dark, dusty corners of the soul, waiting to reemerge. Even those people who are not role-players or readers of fantasy and science fiction have felt it. There arises sometimes a feeling that this world is no longer adequate. There must be something deeper, something more. It is, perhaps, a spiritual desire. Many of us turn to the fantastical, saying, "If only I were Luke Skywalker..." or "If I could just live in Middle-earth..." or "If only I could be as noble and strong as Merlin, or Gandalf."

One reader of fantasy answers my question, "Would you like to be part of those worlds?" with, "God, yeah," and says, "What we do every day is nothing." When I ask him what it is that fantasy characters have that he does not, he answers, "Power," and follows it up with, "It has to be more than what I am" (Sleen 1998). Role-players answer that their characters have magic, charisma, knowledge, power, abilities, and so forth. It is behavior we wish we could restore. One gamer answers, "[The characters] usually know something you don't" (Smith 1998). They do know something that we do not. It is something that we want to know, that we feel we have to know. We pursue them in order to find that knowledge. They hold within their minds something that we know will satisfy our deepest desires. We love them and desire with all our hearts to pass through the wardrobe doors and find a country that, although we have never seen it, we know to be more real, and somehow more true than our own.

The question, of course, is how we get to that truth. To satisfy our desires we immerse ourselves in fantasy novels, letting them carry us away into other lands for a while. Gamers make it as real as possible by means of role-playing the characters whom they experience only vicariously in novels or films. Thus, we satisfy our desires by means of our imagination. After all, it is from our imagination that these images first appeared.

Is there something escapist about this process? Perhaps many people think so. I myself have labeled my fantasy books by saying things like, "Oh, I read that when I need an escape." One gamer excused his response to me, saying, "It sounds pretty close to lapsing into a childhood fantasy, I know..." (Thompson 1998). Is it really all that simple, though? Many people believe gamers are all freaks and that reading a fantasy novel is somehow akin to reading a trashy romance novel. It is true that there is badly written fantasy and science fiction, but there is badly written literature in every genre. Something makes fantasy different. There seems to be an element of fear involved. In *Dungeons & Dragons*, when I first took up the dice to roll my character's strengths, when I began my sketch of her in pencil on heavy brown paper (while the old picnic table, the summer night, and the bugs were all very much of this world too), I have to admit, I felt a twinge of fear. I had heard rumors about *D&D*, rumors of getting too far into the mind of the character, rumors of death, of it altering your mind.

In a collection of her essays, *The Language of the Night* (1979), Le Guin writes about human interactions with fantasy: "[American men] have learned to repress their imagination, to reject it as something childish or effeminate, unprofitable, and probably sinful" (37). The imagination is repressed and seen as nothing more than child's play, to be discarded when one is older. But even when it is for children, people make an effort to make sure it is not real. "'Well, I thought [*Doctor Who*] was scary for the little ones, yeah. You really need to sit with them when they're only small to watch anything like that, so you can tell them, oh, you know, 'this isn't a scary monster, it's just a rubber mask,' and you know, you can interpret for them and then they're not so scared" (Tulloch and Jenkins 1995:109).

This is all very well. We do not want to terrify children. Nevertheless, perhaps there is something profoundly lacking in a culture in which all of the monsters are explained away. To do that is more of a lie than to offer them as a real part of the world. I do not think that when people sat around campfires recounting myths, they would then turn to the children and say, "This isn't real, you know." Because, of course, they knew the sense in which it was. It is up to us to relearn how it is real. Learning that begins with that raw feeling of desire that struck me like a chord in that unprofessional, unsophisticated game around the picnic table by a lake where the only two truths I felt were my deepest desires in that moment: the warmth of a boy's arm brushing against mine, and that small, living hope that I could somehow be the character I played. "Fantasy is the language of the inner self. I will claim no more for fantasy than to say that I personally find it the appropriate language in which to tell stories to children — and others," Le Guin contends (1979:66).

She further states that, while we do wish to teach children about good and evil, it would be immoral to show them pictures of "the gas chambers of Dachau, or the famines of India, or the cruelties of a psychotic parent" (1979:66). She knows that we cannot tell children that there are solutions to these problems, but we also cannot make them bear the weight of the world. It is also wrong to overprotect them. There is evil in the world as well as good. To hide that is, in itself, an act of cruelty. To learn about good and evil through myth is a very healthy way to learn. It is an appropriate language to teach all of us, at any time in our lives. In fact, I doubt there is any better way. My mother read me *The Lord of the Rings* (1954–1955, 1965) when I was quite young, and before that was *The Lion, the Witch and the Wardrobe* (1950). These stories taught me more about the truth of my world and about humanity than anything else. They taught me about pain and joy, about the tests of living, about the dangers of knowledge, and its joys. They taught me about myself and those around me. Moreover, searching for the world of fantasy is more than an escape simply because there is more than an element of truth to it. "For fantasy is true, of course. It isn't factual, but it is true. Children know that. Adults know it too, and that is precisely why many of them are afraid of fantasy" (Le Guin 1979:40).

We all know that we are not going to stumble on a dragon when we next set foot outside. No wizard is going to show up at our little round door and send us on a quest. And the back wall of our wardrobe is not going to suddenly evaporate, revealing a magic world of snow. Admittedly, there are rumors that stranger things have happened, but that is beyond the point. If you have ever read a fantasy novel, you will have found that, despite magic spells and swords, fantasy characters really do not have it much better than we do. In fact, you would probably curse your fate if you landed in even some of the milder situations they find themselves in. Main characters are constantly being torn away from friends and family to do deeds they would really rather not do. There is killing, torture, and carnage. There is pain, grief, and loss on a constant basis. What do they have that we want so much? And why is there such a huge group of people who want it?

Fantasy and science-fiction readers and gamers are not stupid or easily fooled. In fact, they are often quite intelligent. "The majority of people who read science-fiction and fantasy on a regular basis are extremely well-educated. Even if they had not had the benefit to go on to college or graduate school, they are thinkers and they make you toe the line on storytelling a lot stronger than people who are into other types of material" (Killick 1998:3). Most adult gamers have not only received a college education, but have graduate degrees as well. In addition, their imagination seems to be functioning better than a lot of other people (Fine 1983:41–42). No, fantasy and science-fiction fans are not a group of people who simply desire to escape and have the wool pulled over their eyes. These people know what they are doing. They are intellectually intelligent. What is it these stories hold for readers and gamers that is so desirable? It is something that has nothing at all to do with the intellect.

These stories have something we are quite lacking in, and that is the quest. On it, the distinctions between good and evil and battles to be fought become quite clear. It is the ritualization of the soul's desire to know itself. What must be done is laid out. Difficult to accomplish, no doubt, but laid out. The path is set and the only honorable thing to do is to follow it. Through trials, battles, and tests, the quest defines the self of the hero who fights the dragon out in the open, with a result of life or death. In a world in which things are never clear and there is never a choice that can be strictly categorized as good or evil, when the results of a decision are never clearly win or lose, is it any wonder that the simplicity of fantasy is attractive? There is a simplicity of behavior in fantasy that explains to us what can be accomplished in our own lives.

One role-player, Joshua Smith, said, "I enjoy creating the world of my dreams (or more often my nightmares), and watching how myself and others cope with it" (1998). There is something about fantasy that is deeply relevant to ourselves. To confront our own nightmares is the ultimate hero's journey. When we read about a quest or imagine ourselves on one while playing a role-playing adventure, we open paths in our minds and become open to our dreams and ourselves. As Campbell says, if your dreams are in sync with society, then you will live in harmony with it. However, if they are not, then "you've got an adventure in the dark forest ahead of you," eventually becoming a "neurotic" when forced to live within a system that does not support your dreams. Such people may, in fact, become heroes, because they are forced "into the world of fire, of original experience," Campbell explains. And the one who has the "courage to face trials and bring a whole new body of possibilities into the field of inter-preted experience for other people to experience — that is the hero's deed" (1991:48–49).

Such is a dream quest, a hero's journey. What we want is that adven-ture. Despite trial and pain, we cry out to enter the dark forest and the world of fire. In a time when dreams and myths were accepted truth, a boy went off into the wilderness to search for his dream and his shadow. If he was unusually fortunate, the boy might have come back as a chief or a shaman. It is a verification of the dream that we do not have today. We all too often cut ourselves off from our dreams and our shadows. We can see this in the belief that fantasy is a child's fairy tale, and that it is imma-ture to be caught up in fantasy as we get older. The truth is that the fairy tale is the child's fantasy, and as we get older, our fantasies get older. They are not meant to vanish with age, but to change like everything else. Fan-tasy is a way of looking for what is true and false in ourselves and in the world. Fear of the fantastic comes, in many ways, from a fear of the truth about the self and the world.

Myths give us a deeper understanding of the world. They were always meant to, from the original stories, "In the beginning…" Through this understanding of the world, we discover that we are being lead on a quest, and this quest is a journey of the soul. We can escape ourselves for a while and become something else, something with more power, more charisma, anything that makes us "more." But through that reading, or gaming, through that playing out of the myth, we discover what is really true in ourselves, what is already within us that is the "more" that we desire. For example, one gamer said, "Every [character] has a little bit of me" (Aus-lan 1998). The truth is, we have a little bit of each character in us.

Heroes always have battles within themselves as well as in the out-side world. Myths recognize the duality of the world. There is evil and there is good. There is knowledge and there is ignorance. There is the eagle and there is the serpent. And that duality exists just as strongly inside the human mind and heart as it does in the outside world. There is this fear of accepting the knowledge that these myths make it possible for us to realize, almost as though that knowledge were wrong. "Why was the knowledge of good and evil forbidden to Adam and Eve? Without that knowledge, we'd all still be a bunch of babies still in Eden, without any participation in life. Woman brings life into the world" (Campbell 1991:54). Perhaps God intended for the fruit to be eaten. Good and evil had to come to them at some point, but first they had to desire it, and that desire came from the small shred that broke the unity of the garden and made it more interesting — the serpent. Eve recognized this difference, probably sensed his wisdom, and was intrigued by that small sense of difference. And so she willingly entered into the world, not quite prepared for what was to come, but desiring knowledge, which is the real issue here.

I think what intrigues many fans of fantasy and science fiction is the maturing and coming into knowledge that the hero goes through. He or she has to take that plunge, to be able to give up innocence in order to be allowed to gain new knowledge about oneself and the world. And that wisdom is always going to hurt. Knowledge requires painful experience, but it is something that must be dealt with along the way. Audiences are given the hero's chance of knowledge by following along in these mythic tales of truth. There is no way readers can understand *A Wizard of Earthsea*, for example, if they do not take in what it is saying about all of humanity and relate it directly to themselves. We need to connect with the wizard in order to realize that we have that potential as well. What is that potential? It is the ultimate question, "Who am I?" I do not intend to imply that reading fantasy or science fiction or role-playing can answer that question. I am saying that it can begin that process, and it is only a mechanism for becoming the hero and fulfilling the quest.

It is possible for the process of role-playing to lead to self-knowledge. This may seem like a contradiction at first, since it seems that many role-players consider the purpose of creating a character to make it as distant from the self as possible. The question is, "Who am I?" The answer in the imagination and in the role-playing game is, "Anything you bloody well please." To know you can be anything is quite a liberating feeling. Role-players immediately go about adding traits they will never have, and in some cases, traits that it is not possible for anyone to have. Almost all role-players I have talked to include knowledge and power in their list of things that characters have that they themselves do not. There is the player who answered, "It has to be more than what I am." So there is the excitement of knowing that "I can be anything!" It is possible that just this knowledge can lead to knowledge in day-to-day life, but there is more to it than that. In naming their qualities, players are often naming their shadows (I want to point out that not all shadows are evil parts of the self in this particular analysis, simply aspects that we do not or cannot see). When we name things we believe are our opposites, they are often closer to ourselves than we realize. If we say, "I will be a warrior," thinking that we will never ever be a warrior in real life, but feeling a strange desire for it, it is probable that there is a shadow warrior living inside us. When we create this character, the part of the self that wants to be that character surfaces, and we answer through that. We have created a social front, but there is more to the social front than first meets the eye. As Goffman points out, it is not necessarily a charade (1959:19–20). We know if it is a real shadow because instead of leaving when the game is over, it haunts us. Essentially, we have let loose our shadows, and we cannot send them back where they came from, which is the dark world of the unconscious, because they have broken free. We either accept them or let them chase us, turning them into beasts by our unwillingness. This letting free of the shadows begins the quest.

Now that our shadows are out in the open, we embark on the quest. We read books, we play the games, and we watch. We perform using cultural codes, social fronts, and strips of reenacted behavior. Underneath that performance is the hero, ourselves, striving for knowledge. The performance becomes intense. We feel desire and we know that something about what we are doing is true. We play with our shadows, running from them and turning on them, trying to figure out their names, and all this we do through the language of myth. We often must accomplish a surface-level quest. There is a dragon we must kill or some other such deed to be done. It is through this quest that we see clearly the powers of good and evil in the world. We recognize the duality with which all things happen. It is in the process of killing the dragon — not afterwards, but during the heat of the battle — that the knowledge of our own duality comes to us. In the heat of battle, we see our own shadows, and we see ourselves with a clarity that we may never have encountered before. It is in the heat of having to deal with the world's powers that we must deal with our own: "At the bottom of the abyss comes the voice of salvation.... At the darkest moment comes the light" (Campbell 1991:46).

In the pits of darkness, we kill the dragon, and it is in that darkness that we must turn and give a name to the shadow. Like the wizard in Le Guin's novel, we recognize that it dwells within us and find that the name for that demon is our own name. If we can bear that fight and if we can bear to name our outcast dreams, then we begin to fulfill our need. The serpent and the eagle will melt together, and we shall take to the sky!

PART II

Performing the Myth of Science Fiction's Popular Culture Icons

The Mythology of the Stanley Kubrick Image

BY CHRISTINE WITMER

Stars and celebrities are created and adored throughout the world. The late Stanley Kubrick, director of such films as *2001: A Space Odyssey* (1968), *A Clockwork Orange* (1971), *The Shining* (1980), *Full Metal Jacket* (1987), and *Eyes Wide Shut* (1999), was a particular celebrity who still is the focus of much adulation and controversy, shown by many to be a mysterious, meticulous "control freak." However, it is possible to analyze these qualities as themes and tropes that are re-performed in various sites of popular culture in order to prove that they represent a performance of the Stanley Kubrick image or myth, and not necessarily the core truth of the man. Perhaps the image of Stanley Kubrick continues to be created as a representation by others through certain "linguistic codes" present in biographies dedicated to him. These tropes create a kind of "social front"— as explicated by Goffman — that many accept as constituting his true self. These social fronts are translated into various "strips of behavior," as Schechner might say, that then become re-performed in the wider culture, including web pages and other fan representations of Kubrick's man/myth image.

Through the process of semiotics— the reading of inherent symbols— we can examine a biography on Stanley Kubrick to uncover the codes hidden beneath the surface. Words are powerful tools containing hidden meanings in words or phrases buried in the text, sounds, and visual images we get every day from the world around us, affecting us so greatly that they actually construct our perception of the "real." The goal is to examine what subconscious information is being created, to find "the forms, the codes which make meanings possible" (Barthes 1985:84). The codes serve as metaphors for larger events, bigger meanings, and hidden agendas. With or without our knowledge, they permeate our thoughts and influence our minds through literature. Though the two do not seem to mesh, actually literature and performance feed directly into one another. In order to see how something is performed, we must first approach it from some direction of society, influence, or standing. Semiotics offers the perfect opportunity to rationalize writing (in this case, biographies) and shed light on the means by which a social distinction was created for one by another.

In *Stanley Kubrick: A Biography* (1997) by Vincent LoBrutto, many allusions to Kubrick's mysticism can be seen. The author states outright in the prologue, entitled "The Myth of the Reclusive Auteur," that "Like Greta Garbo, Howard Hughes, J.D. Salinger, and Thomas Pynchon, Stanley Kubrick is a celebrated recluse. Kubrick's notorious secrecy, obsessive perfectionism, and ever widening chasm between films have created a torrent of apocryphal stories, producing a mythology more than a man" (1). LoBrutto further elaborates on Kubrick's image as "an intense, cool, misanthropic cinematic genius who obsesses over every detail, a man who lives a hermetic existence, doesn't travel, and is consumed with phobic neuroses" (1). The author then claims that "This book began with the search to understand the man who arguably may be the greatest living film director" (1).

To begin the analysis, the author begins by listing a number of "celebrated recluses." He mentions glamorous ones, putting into use a social code of "fame." These names conjure up the image of famous people living a glory-filled life of solitude. Instead of listing a bunch of not-so-well-known people, he begins with a movie star (Greta Garbo), elevating Kubrick to a higher level of fame. He is careful to mention people whom the American public have accepted for their genius, rather than the ones chastised for their lack of exposure. He could have mentioned less popular recluses who are thought to be weird or dangerously nonsocial; instead, he chooses to glamorize Kubrick and place him into a category of those who are on the outskirts of society and liked by the public all the more for it.

Next, LoBrutto lists Kubrick's "traits," giving the reader no room to disagree. Instead of stating the traits as possibilities of Kubrick, the author uses a linguistic code of form and creates a list telling the reader what, apparently, Kubrick is like. He even states the traits as common knowledge by using the word "notorious." By choosing this word he is playing on the social code of "the bandwagon." He makes it seem that everyone knows Kubrick is like this, so if the reader does not then he or she must be missing something. In an attempt to know what others do, the reader has little choice but to simply agree.

In the mind of the reader, there is no choice whether or not to agree with LoBrutto's assertions. The author then acknowledges that these traits together have made Kubrick somewhat of a myth in culture. By conceding Kubrick's larger-than-life appearance, LoBrutto tries through this linguistic code to convince the reader that he knows more than he really does. He makes the concession, showing that he recognizes the incredulity of the persona, but that he, nonetheless, knows and accepts it as true, as should the reader. By saying Kubrick has done few movies in his life, LoBrutto makes a distinction between laziness and creative genius. In a world in which quantity is important, the author uses the phrase "ever widening chasm between films" to evoke images of great canyons made by God himself. By distinguishing Kubrick as godlike in this linguistic code, the reader is unable to compare him on human terms as one who needs to make more movies. It is clear that, as you would not rush God in his creation, so should you not rush Kubrick. Continuing with the theme, LoBrutto charges Kubrick with causing "a torrent of apocryphal stories" and depicts Kubrick as a veritable force of nature capable of predicting even the end of the world. The author returns to the list format once again, presenting the reader with a number of traits with the appearance of truth. LoBrutto, again, leaves the reader no choice but to believe his assertions by not commenting on them, but rather stating them point-blank as true.

LoBrutto makes himself more human and therefore more trustworthy, in the next sentence, when he uses the word "may" instead of "is" in regard to what Kubrick could be like in real life. He uses the societal code that people are more willing to believe those who can admit they are wrong. In the mind of the reader, he must be speaking the truth because if he were wrong he would be sure to just admit it himself. He also, in the next sentence, uses the word "arguably" when speaking of Kubrick's reputation, in stark contrast to the blatant unproven statements he was making in the previous sentence. As seen in this passage, LoBrutto masters the art of manipulation when he clearly tricks the reader into believing his assertions about Kubrick. In this short passage, LoBrutto has already created a persona of Kubrick by manipulating the reader's intrinsic set of cultural tropes to make them translate his words into truths. He has created Kubrick as a godlike man whose creative genius all but forces him to reject society and pursue cinematic perfection with the solitude of his camera lens. This is the "social front" that, according to Goffman, is the self that gets performed, while the "real attitudes, beliefs, and emotions of the individual can be ascertained only indirectly" (1959:2). Stanley Kubrick's social front is perpetuated by others through linguistic codes found in his biographies. He is constructed as a man with many faces, a meticulous perfectionist, a hopeless recluse, a man who has no care for humanity.

These traits, expressed in *Stanley Kubrick: A Biography*, did give Kubrick some benefits. It could be argued that this specific social front served him well. In many ways, he received a pristine privacy that is often lacked by celebrities with his caliber of fame. Whereas other filmmakers may feel pressure to put out a number of films within a certain number of years, the godlike Kubrick was allowed complete freedom as to how many films he wanted to make (indeed, it was a dozen years between *Full Metal Jacket* and *Eyes Wide Shut*). Since he was reputed as being such a genius needing all the time, support, and funds to make his masterpieces (of apocalyptic proportions according to LoBrutto), he was allowed to have almost total control over his films while, at the same time, keeping everyone else in the dark. This can be seen in his final film, *Eyes Wide Shut* (1999). In accordance with his social front, he took a painstakingly long time to shoot this movie (perfectionism), shot it in a foreign country (presumably to maintain privacy), swore his cast to secrecy (to preserve his masterpiece's anonymity), and created the whole drama without the producing studio's ever really knowing what the movie was about. Indeed, it is not necessary to bother Kubrick with petty details such as plot summary, for according to LoBrutto, he is a genius whose godlike productions are paralleled only by Mother Nature herself. His myth allowed for a huge "hype" to follow the pre-release of this film. Rumors were created as the anticipation mounted to see what this man, who shrouds his films in secrets, would do next. His social front was solely responsible for these allowances, which, for any other director, would be unheard of. Kubrick's myth/social front allowed him to achieve his own goals, unbothered and in unheard-of privacy and secrecy.

Through Schechner's restoration of behavior theory—in which "strips of behavior" are seen as material that can be "rearranged or reconstructed" (1985:35)—it can, perhaps, be argued that websites offer a new place where the myth of Stanley Kubrick gets re-performed. For example, at the website *www.doc-h.demon.co.uk/shining.htm*, the interface between the audience and Kubrick's myth appears, where one can see the "strips of behavior" or traits of his myth, being re-performed. Visitors to this site replay, through access to text, pictures, and sound bites, pieces of Kubrick's myth. The visitor is allowed to re-perform Kubrick's movies, creations, and invented persona through the interface of this website. This particular site opens with a plain white background and very little text. The site contains many pictures of Kubrick, presumably from when he was filming *The Shining*. In the pictures, he is featured complete with a full, dark, bushy beard and dark, bushy eyebrows. The pictures, none smiling, are brooding, capturing him deep in thought, at a typewriter, and with a fanatical look as he grasps a camera. These strips of behavior portray the myth of his indelible dark side. He is alone in the majority of the pictures, replaying and reinforcing his image as a recluse intensely needing solitude.

Another ideal example of his myth's re-performance at this site is through the sound bite entitled "Kubrick Loses Temper with Shelley Duvall." It consists of Kubrick giving direction to Duvall and quarreling over her interpretation of a line reading. This "strip of behavior" and no other was chosen to perpetuate Kubrick's myth as being a man who, because of his genius and lack of social graces, is hard to get along with. Through this performance, he is seen as a recluse who cannot get along with real people, but rather would choose the company only of a camera lens. In this site where Kubrick is king, Shelley Duvall is cast as the person who fails to recognize the Kubrick's greatness and therefore needs to be put in her place. Through the touch of a button, the visitor is able to retrieve and replay a portion of Kubrick's real voice, seemingly incontrovertible evidence of his social front. By the chosen bite of sound itself, and the virtue of its content, his myth is reinforced and re-performed for the visitor.

Stanley Kubrick was a man of mystery for sure, but whose ingenuity can we credit for creating this persona that is both mysterious and likable, stubborn but successful, and feared but respected? This man of intense popularity has been analyzed by many people. We see that the creation is derived from the linguistic codes found in biographies on him that create his social front. The social front is not without benefits, for it allowed him to create films at any rate and with unfettered support from his producers.

In a posthumous perpetuation of Kubrick's image, during the Director's Guild Association's memorial service for the late director on May 16, 1999, Vincent D'Onofrio was quoted as giving the following anecdote about the filming of *Full Metal Jacket* (1987): "They were shooting the scene in Vietnam where the men in Joker's platoon are being picked off one by one by a sniper. [I] was on the set to observe and noticed that a van had pulled up and was watching the filming from some distance away. They had been there for awhile when he finally asked the First Assistant Director who the people sitting in the van were. Kubrick overheard the query and replied, 'Those are the London film executives. They're not allowed to get out'" (*www.aint-it-cool-news.com*).

The Performance
of George Pal

BY SNEZHANA KUSHNIR

George Lucas, Steven Spielberg, and Gene Roddenberry may have been unable to achieve their great success and creativity if George Pal had not paved the way for them. In the 1950s and 1960s, no one devoted so much effort and imagination to the making of science-fiction (SF) films as Pal. He was a producer/director beyond his time who ignited the imagination of moviegoers with fantastic tales of adventure and exploration. This visionary captured the attention of the animation and special effects industries with his Puppetoons and stop-action photography. Such creations, which were never seen before, brought him recognition and moved him closer toward live-action films. His first film, *Destination Moon* (1951), chronicled humanity's trip to the moon and foreshadowed the actual moon landing nearly two decades before it actually happened. Perhaps it is not completely outrageous to consider how Pal's creation helped inspire our drive toward the moon. After *Destination Moon*, many other science-fiction classics followed: *When Worlds Collide* (1951), *The War of the Worlds* (1953), and *The Time Machine* (1960) to name just a few. All of his hard work and creativity scored him several Academy Awards for Best Special Effects and have been the inspiration for many people in corresponding fields. George Pal was a science-fiction guru whose mind and relentless dedication to fantasy have helped make the world of SF filmmaking as captivating as it is today.

George Pal was born in Cegléd, Hungary, into a theatrical family on February 1, 1908. At first he intended to become an architect while studying at the Budapest Academy, but after taking illustration classes his true love and talent in creative drawing emerged. Although he ended up graduating with an architecture degree, the lack of opportunity for architects in Hungary led him to take a job at Hunnia, a small Hungarian film studio, where he worked as an animation illustrator. When Pal learned that the job was an unpaid apprenticeship, he and his wife, Zsoka, moved to Berlin, where he found work at UFA (the famous German studio that was home to such legendary filmmakers as Fritz Lang, the director of the 1926 film *Metropolis*). Although Pal supervised all of the studio's cartoon production after only two months, the Pals were forced to flee Germany and move to Prague, Czechoslovakia, in order to escape Hitler's Gestapo. In Prague, Pal tried to start up his own animation company, but he could not find any of the equipment he needed. So, instead of cartoons, he decided to use puppets, leading to his development of his Puppetoons, puppet creations that changed the world of animation forever.

Pal's Puppetoons took him and his wife from Paris to Einhover, Holland, where the animator found a studio and had much success with his creations. After catching the attention of American producers, and while teaching at Columbia University, Pal signed a contract with Paramount Pictures, where he produced dozens of "non-advertising Puppetoon shorts" (Martin 1998:90). In no time, Pal was working with the best animators in the field, including Wah Chang, Gene Warren, Bob Baker, and Ray Harryhausen. Quickly, Pal became a hot Hollywood commodity, and in 1950 Paramount gave him the green light to produce his first live-action film, *Destination Moon*.

This film was "widely considered to be the first [SF] movie of the 'Red Scare' era, when futuristic films, created as a subtle reminder of the threat of global communism and nuclear annihilation and man's ability to stave off these impending dooms through science and technology, were in full bloom" (Martin 1998:98). Next came another SF classic, *When Worlds Collide*. This film, like *Destination Moon*, won Pal an Oscar for Best Special Effects. All the attention and interest that came from the success of these films allowed Pal to continue his fantastic filmmaking and develop movies like *War of the Worlds* (the film that has brought him the most recognition), *Tom Thumb* (1958), *The Wonderful World of the Brothers Grimm* (1962), and *The Seven Faces of Dr. Lao* (1963).

George Pal's genius was the key that unlocked the entrance to a world of endless possibilities and fantasy. That same genius is why he is still performed in such popular culture as websites, memorabilia, and articles. He is best-known for his innovations, which have changed the meaning and respect given to science-fiction films. The mythic image of George Pal — like strips of Schechner's behavior getting restored in new forms — continues to be re-performed on websites dedicated to him.

For instance, a web page at *www.scifistation.com* has a section dedicated to George Pal. The page opens with "The Fantasy Film Worlds of George Pal." Underneath the title is a list of subjects: Purchase, The Making of, Pal Bio, Scenes, The Legacy, ObFacts, Home. Further down, in large italicized letters, we read, "Before Spielberg … Before Lucas … There Was George Pal." The page gives information about the filmmaker, such as his date of birth and death, the number of films he worked on, and so forth. After clicking on the Purchase page, a few paragraphs about The Fantasy Film Worlds of George Pal appears, along with a picture on the cover of the video box documentary. After providing pertinent ordering information, the page estimates the number of weeks that it takes for the video to arrive and wishes the purchaser a pleasant viewing.

The "Making of" page first appears with pictures from the movie. The first image is of a scientist in a lab coat looking straight into the camera and in front of a table full of scientific gadgets. Underneath the photo are a couple of sentences describing the shot. Moving farther down the page, there is a photo of the Martian spaceship used in *War of the Worlds* and a description of the shot beneath it. This continues throughout the entire page in this section. After opening the "Pal Bio" page, several paragraphs appear describing his life and work. Running along the left side of the screen are pictures of him. The first picture on the upper left side is an image of a smiling Pal in a tux. The other pages are set up in a similar fashion. There are paragraphs of information on either the man or his inventions, while different photos appear alongside the words. The site itself is a reenactment of the man as well as his life and products. It takes events and actions that have already occurred and re-performs them in a new context — a "restoration of behavior." This performance continues as people log onto the site.

Whenever fans collect George Pal memorabilia, whether it is a poster of him (in which he is surrounded by his Puppetoons, all done in black and white) or one of his films (a bright Technicolor picture from *The Time Machine*) or a model of a Martian spaceship (which has a flat, round body and a long, giraffe-like neck of sparkling metal), they are taking a certain moment or "strip" from the life and work of Pal and re-performing it on their own. As Schechner contends, "performers get in touch with, recover, remember, or even invent these strips of behavior, and then rebehave according to these strips" (1985:36). A fan may purchase a poster of *War of the Worlds* with bright eye-catching colors, depicting people running away from spaceships firing laser beams. Every time they view that poster, they reenact an image originally created by George Pal. Through this very process, Pal gets re-performed in popular culture images. Articles that have been and are still being written about Pal are also a form of restored behavior. Erik J. Martin's "King George" in *Cinescape Magazine* takes the natural event of Pal's existence and transforms it into a kind of written performance — the writer shaping strips of various Pal "behaviors" in any way the writer pleases, whether that is an expression or an absence of historical data and the shaping of opinions about Pal and his life.

Most notably, the most involved examples of restored behavior in the performance of George Pal are the influences of his innovations. From his Puppetoons to his drive for better special effects and love of fantasy, his work ripples out into the inspiration of others' achievements that otherwise may not have existed. Pal's use of single-frame photography, stop-motion animation, and replacement figure puppets in his Puppetoons caught the eye of every animator. The combination of inanimate objects filmed as cartoons brought realism to animation that was never seen before on that high of a level. This inspired Walt Disney to develop his animation department and make his cartoons as believable and realistic as possible. In fact, Disney was a close friend of Pal's and would sometimes ask him for advice. Pal's puppets were an influence in the building of Disneyland in exhibits like "It's a Small World" (*scifistation.com*). Disney's team of animators studied Pal's Puppetoons, according to Ward Kimball, creator of Jiminy Cricket. Walt was so fascinated because he strove to attain three-dimensionality in his animation and Pal was doing it right before his eyes.

Claymation also came about from the invention of Puppetoons, and although Pal used a different type of wood model, his "strip of behavior" is obviously altered into its own performance. The technique of stop-motion animation was used in every one of Pal's films in one form or another. "This technique is where it all started and the same basic process is the building block of all CGI [computer graphics image] today from *Jurassic Park* to *Toy Story*" (Martin 1998).

Pal's brilliance caused the restoration of his ideas over and over again. Robert Wise was influenced by *Destination Moon* when making *The Day the Earth Stood Still* (1951). And Gene Roddenberry, who had his offices across the hall from Pal at Paramount Studios, would come to Pal for advice on the making of his highly regarded 1960s *Star Trek* television series. Moreover, Pal inspired countless artists, writers, and filmmakers, who, in turn, inspired scientists and astronauts, whose amazing journeys into space during the past thirty years inspired a whole new generation of science-fiction creators. The continual restoration of Pal's behavior is what led and continues to lead to new performances, which in turn lead to other performances. The performance of Pal will probably never end. Not only has it penetrated, shaped, and influenced the SF film world, but also anything and anyone that has to do with fantasy, fiction, space, and beyond. We have taken Pal's behavior and have repeatedly restored it, and will continue to do so, whether we are conscious of it or not.

George Lucas:
His Roles and His Myths

BY STEVE BEBOUT

When *Star Wars* was released in 1977, George Lucas's place as a Hollywood contender was confirmed. This was Lucas's second blockbuster, preceded by his 1973 hit, *American Graffiti*, which he directed and co-wrote and which was an enormous financial success. *Star Wars* and the legacy that followed, however, far exceeded the success of *American Graffiti* and the expectations of a simple kid from rural northern California. Since then, Lucas has become one of the most important and influential people in the film industry. Although he maintains a high status in Hollywood, he has made every attempt to stay out of the "Hollywood spotlight," directing only four films in a thirty-year career. Lucas and those around him have shaped Lucas's image as an independent, creative, and untainted artist. His personal feelings about the "biz" have influenced the persona Lucas projects to the public, which has almost always been focused on his work.

When someone projects a certain persona, Goffman explains, "he implicitly requests his observers to take seriously the impression that is fostered before them" (1959:17). Goffman believes that everyone assumes a character and goes through life performing and inhabiting that character. Hollywood is the perfect place to see this theory played out. There are many characters in Hollywood — many celebrities who create specific public images. Although he would not consider himself the Hollywood type, George Lucas is no exception.

Lucas has managed to create a rather interesting role for himself as a filmmaker. Although he has access to large amounts of money and institutional power, he comes across as an independent film director and writer. This role is created in several ways. Lucas speaks consistently about his discontent with the Hollywood system and the people who make up that system. "I think some of the people in the movie business are sleazy and unscrupulous, and I would say probably the majority are that bad," Lucas commented in an interview. Lucas takes great pride in the fact that he makes his films outside Hollywood, "where people make movies, not deals" (Pollock 1990:5). These ideals reflect those of an independent film artist. Of course, unlike most independent directors, Lucas can afford to take this stance. His film company, Lucasfilm, Ltd., is a thriving company of which Lucas is the boss, and he needs little outside support from studios. In 1990, Lucas and his friend Steven Spielberg, whom he collaborated with on the *Indiana Jones* films, had eight of the ten highest-grossing films of all time, an outstanding achievement for an "independent film artist."

Most of the time, George Lucas keeps away from the spotlight and the media. This privacy helps to perpetuate his image. Lucas grants few interviews and comes out only to talk about new works or to speak as a leader in the film community. Unlike Spielberg, who is probably the best comparison as a commercial counterpart to Lucas, Lucas does not appear on talk shows or in news magazines. He keeps his appearances minimal and talks about his work, not his personal life.

Lucas's role as an independent artist is also reflected in his "costume." He has maintained the simple, guy-next-door, Sunday-afternoon father look. He does not look like a typical Hollywood mogul. In production photos from the sets of his films, Lucas is usually wearing an old pair of jeans and a flannel shirt. Then, of course, there is the scruffy beard. As insignificant as it may seem, Lucas's "costume" supports the role that he is presenting to the public. In fact, the name George Lucas has become synonymous with *Star Wars*. The *Star Wars* series is embedded in our popular culture, and George Lucas is the man behind it all.

After Lucas was finished with *American Graffiti*, he began working on his new, rather large idea. Lucas researched everything from science fiction to fairy tales, trying, he has said, "to get fairy tales, myths, and religion down to a distilled state, studying the pure form to see how and why it worked" (Pollock 1990:134). Lucas had a difficult time getting his ideas down on paper, so he began by writing a synopsis of the plot. The project was eventually picked up by Fox, and Lucas went to work on the script. Lucas used many archetypal characters and plot lines in the construction of *Star Wars*. The major influence of *Star Wars*, however, was another Lucas film: *THX 1138* (1971). Lucas used many of the same ideas and characters from this film: the robot policemen from *THX* become storm troopers in *Star Wars*, the OMM is much like the Emperor, and the one who makes his escape and faces the unknown has become Luke Skywalker (Pollock 1990:142). *Star Wars* was an instant success, and it left its stamp on America. George Lucas became the father of one of the biggest pop-culture phenomena. With uncanny prescience and business acumen, Lucas knew that *Star Wars* was too big for just one movie. He secured the rights to the sequels in his original contract with Fox, and began his work on the rest of the story which he knew would take two more films.

After the original *Star Wars*, Lucas immediately began work on the second film, *The Empire Strikes Back* (1980). This time, however, Lucas, who wrote the story line, did not write the screenplay. Instead, he hired Leigh Brackett. Brackett completed the first draft of the screenplay and passed away two weeks later. Lucas then began to work on the script himself, hiring Lawrence Kasdan, who later wrote the script for the Spielberg/Lucas venture *Raiders of the Lost Ark* (1981). Lucas also relieved himself of the directing position for this movie by hiring Irvin Kershner. Lucas put a great deal of faith in Kershner. He told him, "You know, the second part of this series is the most important one. If it works, then we'll make a third and maybe a fourth. If it doesn't work, it'll be old hat and it'll destroy the real bloom on the project. So it's all up to you!" Lucas's involvement with *Empire* was much different from his tireless work on *Star Wars*. Lucas was not even there when the shooting began. He said, "I thought I'd stand back and see how everything falls apart because I'm not there. And it didn't" (Pollock 1990:214). Lucas maintained daily telephone contact with Kershner but was not closely involved with the live action of the film (216). He did supervise the special effects work at ILM (Industrial Light and Magic), but his role in the production of this film was not as big as the general public believes. Lucas was actually unhappy with some of the work on *Empire* as well as its bulging budget. He commented, "It looks pretty because Kersh took a lot of time to do it. It's a great luxury that we couldn't afford. And ultimately it doesn't make that much difference" (217–218).

Lucas was more involved with the third installment of the *Star Wars* trilogy: *Return of the Jedi* (1983). He co-wrote the screenplay with Kasdan and had *Jedi* directed by Richard Marquand. However, Lucas did spend much more time on the set during this film to make sure that the financial problems that occurred during *Empire* did not return. Ironically, despite Lucas's smaller involvement on the last two films, many are convinced that he directed all three motion pictures. This assumption is often supported in the media and by his fans. When the special edition trilogy was released in 1997, the trailer for all three movies said that the new releases were "George Lucas's definitive vision." Although they are his plot lines and his characters, the "definitive vision" is usually that of the director, not the executive producer. Another interesting statement in the trailer for the new releases is, "In 1977, Producer/Director George Lucas created the *Star Wars* trilogy and changed the way we looked at movies." George Lucas *is* the creator of the *Star Wars* legacy, but the wording of this statement is a bit misleading. He did not create the trilogy in 1977. He had a plot structure for the next two films, but the trilogy was not completed, and by no means was it fully written. And Lucas did not create *Star Wars* by himself; he had considerable help.

To fully explore Goffman's theory about the "presentation of self," one must look at how Lucas's role affects people. How is Lucas perceived? The World Wide Web is an interesting place to look for George Lucas in performance. There are many sites based on *Star Wars* and many based on Lucas himself. On the web, Lucas assumes an almost godlike role. The main page of the *George Lucas Home Page* (*www.geocities.com/Hollywood/ Boulevard/1805/lucass.html*) reads: "For those of you who have visited my website before, you'll notice there's been a drastic change in the look of this place. I hope it is better, because I believe George deserves only the best. Though I have always enjoyed his work, it was only last year when I rediscovered the wonderful universe and story he created out of so little." Praise of Lucas like this is consistent throughout the World Wide Web. While most celebrities' sites contain pictures, biographical information, and trivia, the sites about Lucas are consistently about the work — especially *Star Wars* — and not about his personal life.

Most of the *Star Wars* sites on the internet have a section within the site dedicated to Lucas. His name always goes with the movie. This is not completely strange, considering he did dream up the story. However, there are few other film sites where the creator plays such a large role. At first glance, the main logo for *Ben & Grover's Star Wars Homepage* appears to be a collage of a bunch of different characters and scenes from *Star Wars*. Upon closer examination, one can see that a picture of Lucas is in the background. His face covers nearly the entire logo. It is like the face of God with all of his creatures surrounding him. There are several pictures of Lucas sitting in studios surrounded by models and miniatures from the films, always looming over his creations. Although Lucas did not make the models or create Darth Vader's costume depicted here, he is, without question, the god of the *Star Wars* universe.

George Lucas is an interesting man who plays two main roles in his public life: he is a serious filmmaker and the creator of *Star Wars*. These roles are played out in many different ways. Lucas is certainly aware of these roles, but he does not seem to be the one in control. His fans have created a godlike figure, and Lucas is apparently just along for the ride. This simple man would surely never think of himself as a god, but to many, of course, he is.

The Myth of George Lucas Surrounding The Phantom Menace

BY ROBERT DELANEY

On May 19, 1999, the release of *Star Wars: The Phantom Menace* occurred amid one of the largest "media blitzes" that accompanied any major film sequel (or "prequel," since it covers the previous *Star Wars* background). It was, arguably, one of the most anticipated films of all time. At the helm of this film was George Lucas, unquestionably one of the most influential men in the history of motion pictures. For many, this film granted the opportunity to return to the universe within Lucas's mind which they have longed to explore more deeply. For many others, this film opened the door to Lucas's creative genius for the first time, undoubtedly winning legions of new fans.

Useful in understanding the *Star Wars* phenomenon is an examination of the character and persona of George Lucas himself. It is possible to take a closer look at what may be called the performance of Lucas as propagated and presented in 1998, surrounding the media coverage of the release of *The Phantom Menace*. While one may question Lucas's motives for creating and performing the myth of his own character, one must recognize that they, in fact, do exist. Vision, artistic integrity, economic power, sustenance of a preexisting myth — perhaps all are factors in Lucas's adoption of the role of a great producer and his willingness to let others promulgate it. Rather than speculate, however, we may look at current examples of Lucas's ever-growing myth.

In an interview in a recent issue of *Star Wars Insider* magazine, British actor Hugh Quarshie, who played Captain Panaka in *The Phantom Menace*, offers some insight on the nature of Lucas's myth.

> STAR WARS INSIDER: What about *Star Wars*? Were you a fan when it first came around?
>
> HUGH QUARSHIE: Are you kidding?! I was a huge fan! I was eagerly anticipating it. And I remember insisting we all go to the cinema to see *The Empire Strikes Back* on a big screen with a full bucket of popcorn. Those films offered an experience, a unique cinematic experience. It's one of those things that actually reminds you of your shared humanity — everyone's doing the same thing and enjoying it. Not many films give you that experience these days.
>
> I don't know what goes through George Lucas's mind, but it's a strange combination of being very worldly but also hanging on to something naive in its enthusiasm for youth. (Quarshie 1998)

While the preceding interview sample may seem innocuous enough at first reading, we can see that George Lucas is effectively performing through Quarshie. It is not brain-washing, but consciously or unconsciously, Quarshie is fulfilling and supporting the Lucas myth. Here, I would like to turn to Barthes to help examine some of the codes contained within Quarshie's comments. Goffman's and Barthes's theories are complementary in this instance, as Goffman helps us recognize and understand the performance of a "social front" and Barthes allows us to dissect further and appreciate codes and symbols contained within examples such as Quarshie's interview.

Quarshie says: "Those films offered an experience, a unique cinematic experience." Right away Lucas's films are elevated to higher status. They are personified in that they "offer" something; a transaction takes place between film and audience. A relationship comes into existence as the viewer is in fact receiving something. The word "offer" is different from "give" or "show"; it implies a sense of beneficence or selflessness that we associate with religion or charity.

We may then take a look at what it is the films purport to offer: a "unique cinematic experience. It's one of those things that actually reminds you of your shared humanity." Here, Quarshie invokes codes that are both religious and social. A sense of mystery is instilled when he says, "It's one of those things." It lends an unidentifiable quality, piquing curiosity with its enigmatic nebulosity. What is it? One can only watch, and hope to discover. According to Quarshie, the discovery "actually reminds you of your shared humanity." This is a particularly interesting point, as "shared humanity" represents codes that hint at the basic nature of mythmaking itself. Myths *are* shared humanity and according to Quarshie, myths are what *Star Wars* has to offer. He continues by explaining that "everyone's doing the same thing and enjoying it. Not many films give you that experience these days." Not a "whole bunch" of people or "the majority," but in fact *everyone* is doing the same thing. This puts forth the image of not just a community, but a focused community, with a common goal and a common set of ideals. A quotation like this also plays on the reader psychologically; one may think, "Well, if *everyone* is doing it, I suppose I should too." As much as Quarshie himself trumpets the virtue of being "unique," one certainly would not want to find his or her uniqueness through missing out on the *Star Wars* experience.

Further, Quarshie finishes this train of thought by saying, "I don't know quite what goes through George Lucas's mind, but it's a strange combination of being very worldly but also hanging on to something naive in its enthusiasm for the things of youth." Again an element of mystery is called up. The interview presents Quarshie as an intelligent guy; we learn that he used to be a journalist and that he performed for years at the Royal Shakespeare Company. Before that, he graduated from Oxford with degrees in politics, philosophy, and economics and went on to co-direct the Oxford and Cambridge Shakespeare Companies. Most interesting though, is that for years Quarshie made his living not by acting, but by writing, directing, and producing theater. Lucas is also a writer, director, and producer, and he received his degree in film from the University of Southern California. But when his employee, Hugh Quarshie, whom we know to have a thoroughly admirable career — both academically and artistically — speaks of him, the tone is not just respectful, it is reverent. That Quarshie is so educated and experienced in so many ways only strengthens and validates his praise of Lucas.

The statement that is at the core of Quarshie's performance of Lucas is, "it's a strange combination of being very worldly but also hanging on to something naive in its enthusiasm for the things of youth." Here, Quarshie outlines both the myth of George Lucas and the George Lucas of myth. "Strange combination"? Lucas is presented as something rare and unlikely, heightening his previously described aspect of uniqueness. Also, the following comments are codes that call up images of the wizard and child working together in creative harmony. There is a sort of union within Lucas of seemingly paradoxical forces from which opposite ends of the spectrum meet in a way that inspires awe in "everyone" from the fan in the throng to the seasoned professional whose career is based on the same principle of bringing art to life.

Hugh Quarshie's interview gives us tremendous insight into the nature of Lucas's myth. Application of the theories of Barthes and Goffman help us to delve deeper and gain a better understanding of what is tran-spiring within the interview. We are able to understand that a subtle and carefully engineered performance is taking place, not just a simple "Q and A" session in which a few tidbits about the new *Star Wars* movie get dropped. Exactly how the "players" in this performance are cognizant that they are performing at all is of little consequence. One might argue that there is a degree of performance to every conversation and interaction that takes place on this planet.

In a recent special collector's issue of *Cinescape Insider* magazine, Rick McCallum interviewed George Lucas on location in the Palace Chapel of the Caserta Palace in Italy. The Caserta Palace served as the movie set-ting home of the young Queen Amadila, a character in *The Phantom Men-ace*. Another noteworthy point, which is not stated in the interview, is that interviewer Rick McCallum also happens to be the producer of this film. The title of this interview is "Master of the Jedi."

McCallum's first question to Lucas was: "Many years ago a book was written about the seven directors who control the world. If you had to rewrite it today, would you include yourself and Steven Spielberg?" Lucas responded: "This is only my fourth film as a director, so I'm just a young director, I haven't really come that far." First off, the question itself is at least as interesting as the answer it garners. McCallum recalls a lost tome with a forgotten name that speaks of the "seven directors who control the world." Notably, his reference is not contemporary film, or even Holly-wood, but "the world." Then McCallum calls up the only other director working today with an oeuvre comparable to Lucas's and asks if he feels that they now control the world. Lucas, in turn, shrugs the question off, adopting a modest tone: "I'm just a young director, I haven't really come that far." Lucas unspokenly relies on his audience to try and think of another young director whose films have had such a widespread influence, spanning generations. The juxtaposing images of lofty, world-dominat-ing achievements and homemade fluky success within this question-and-answer unit are a fascinating display of the guidelines of "social front" performance as described by Goffman. McCallum and Lucas's "opposing" points of view successfully paint a picture of an honest craftsman who remains ignorant of the scope of his influence.

Lucas's reverent interviewer continues: "Do you feel responsible for a part of the transformation of cinema due to technology?" Lucas answers affirmatively: "I definitely feel a part of the transformation of cinema. I feel fortunate to be living during this exciting period in filmmaking. It's equivalent to the beginning of cinema or the point when sound was dis-covered or color. Digital technology is a new color for an artist in cinema to expand [the filmmaker's] imagination." Here again, the code of the icon is put forth. More than just a maker of great films, Lucas acknowledges that he is at least partly responsible for a transformation within the art of cinema. However, he equates the recent technological advances in film with the landmark advances of sound and color. He does not, however, acknowledge that his own company, Industrial Light and Magic, is at the forefront of this revolution. Instead, he expresses his gratitude by saying, "I feel fortunate to be living during this exciting period." We see that Lucas is a canny interviewee who takes care to show both sides of the coin.

McCallum cleverly sets up questions that allow Lucas to easily make his major marketing points: "In all the new wave of fantasy movies there is a sort of spiritualism that has taken place inside the plots. Do you feel this is happening in *Star Wars*?" In an attempt to refute the "action movie" stigma, Lucas responds: "Generally what I have heard is that all new movies don't seem to have any heart or soul and that they're all action. I think that *Star Wars* has a heart and soul and goes beyond action." With that type of leading question, Lucas is thereby able to make a blanket statement in which no other new movie can claim to have a "heart or soul." Whether or not Lucas believes the damning statement he makes is debatable. It is an interview; things may seem stronger than intended, and generalization is often employed in daily speech. But, we must remember that Lucas and McCallum have a movie to market. This is a unique interview and one in which the performance of a preexisting myth is readily recognizable due to the similar agendas of the interviewer and interviewee. McCallum knows the exact questions that will shine an endearing light on Lucas. Their complementary use of metaphysical codes like "spiritual" and "soul" elevate their product to another plane of existence, a level which, according to them, one will find in no other film.

In closing, the interviews contained herein take on a far greater significance when examined through the lens of Goffman's and Barthes's studies in performance theory. More than just transactions of information surrounding the making of a film that is unique in the level of excitement it has generated, these interviews can effectively be seen as arenas for the veritable performance of the myth of George Lucas. *Webster's* defines myth as "a traditional story or legend," and in *The Presentation of Self in Everyday Life* (1959) Goffman explains: "Sometimes the traditions of an individual's role will lead him to give a well-designed impression." Put these ideas together and it is evident that an interview is often much more than "meets the eye" or ear. Thus, there is "George Lucas the Man" and there is "George Lucas the Myth." As his own interview indicates, Lucas has learned his myth well and knows how to use it. As the interview with

Hugh Quarshie indicates, much of the rest of the world is intimately familiar with his myth as well. The success of *Star Wars: The Phantom Menace* was the result of a myriad of factors, not the least of which was the performance of the George Lucas's myth.

Star Wars: *The Magic of the Anti-Myth*

BY DANIEL MACKAY

"*Star Wars*: The Magic of Myth" is the Smithsonian's National Air and Space Museum's latest effort to increase the jet stream of visitors passing through its glass doors. It is an exhibition of original production models, props, costumes, and characters used in the first three *Star Wars* features: *A New Hope* (1977), *The Empire Strikes Back* (1980), and *Return of the Jedi* (1983). During this exhibit, visitors behold C-3PO, R2-D2, Chewbacca, Yoda, the Wampa, Jabba's court (complete with Sy Snootles and Salacious B. Crumb), Boba Fett, Wicket, Admiral Ackbar, Darth Vader, a storm trooper and Imperial royal guard, a Jawa and Tusken Raider, and the costumes of Han, Luke, Lando, and Leia. Also included is a fleet of models and vehicles used in the films: a life-size speeder bike with a scout trooper in the saddle, a fifteen-foot-long Mon Calamari transport, the prop of Han Solo frozen in carbonite, an AT-AT, and, a Millennium Falcon, measuring two and a half feet in diameter, built for *Return of the Jedi*, complete with carbon-scorched armor, melted shielding, and (thanks to the merry pranksters at Industrial Light and Magic) a tiny "Champion" spark-plug sticker worn like a license plate across its bow.

Covering the walls are a plethora of original previsualization sketches, storyboards, and paintings, the majority of which were rendered by the conceptual artist for the trilogy, Ralph McQuarrie. The storyboards contain sketches of what each shot in question was intended to look like, along with a breakdown of other elements that would have to be composited into

---

An earlier version of this essay appeared in the journal *Foundation* #76 (Summer 1999).

the shot. Visitors may be surprised at how closely the special effects team at ILM followed these sketches. In *Return of the Jedi*'s final space battle, some shots required up to sixty different elements; it was the storyboard that allowed the ILM cameramen to keep track of these dizzyingly complicated effects.

The effect of displaying the storyboards—which were followed so closely that they almost look like sketches done *after* the film was shot—alongside McQuarrie's paintings, many of which feature settings and scenarios that never made it to the final script stage, incites an endless string of "what-ifs" inside the mind of the visitor. McQuarrie's industrially polished paintings, always dramatic and epic in scope, depict scratched concepts for a Darth Vader Castle, in which the Emperor would appear to Vader in *Empire*. Also hanging on the walls of the exhibit is a painting of a Rebel base set in a grassland version of Monument Valley that was in an early draft of *Jedi*. A pyramid-covered landscape is the setting for another painting, this one of an archaic technological Imperial City slightly reminiscent of the Los Angeles of the future in Ridley Scott's *Blade Runner* (1982). This concept painting would be revisited for the special edition of *Jedi* (1997), in which we are finally treated to a brief glimpse of Coruscant, the Imperial planet/city, during the revised conclusion. Finally, most interesting of all, there are early concept paintings for a duel between Luke Skywalker and Darth Vader in the volcanic bowels of the Emperor's Throne Room, set on a planet pitted with molten lava lakes that stretch out into the infernal horizon.

The exhibit reveals the craftsmanship that went into the making of another world: from deliberately frayed Tatooine-worn desert robes to the knotted and clumped strings of yak hair that make Chewbacca look as if he could bust out of his glass cage and pilot one of the museum's V-2 rockets to some Wookie planet far, far away. For those who dressed up as Princess Leia for Halloween, or Han Solo, Darth Vader, or the cackling Emperor, here is their chance to see how far off they were when struggling to assemble some approximation of what they remembered the characters to be wearing in the film. The illusion these artifacts made when assembled in the films themselves, unified by John Williams's unforgettable score, was more than the sum of its parts, but those parts remain well-crafted icons resonant within the imagination of millions of Americans. The focus of the exhibit is on the art and craftsmanship of the visual designers of the film, and it is in this area that curator Mary Henderson and exhibition designer Linda King focused their talents and produced a rich, evocative presentation.

The great theme of the exhibit is that *Star Wars* is not just an awesome spectacle — an immersive and overwhelming image that transports the visitor to another time and place for a period of two hours. No, visitors are instructed that these films have cultural capital; they are relevant to a "timeless" audience because of their mythological themes. Considering *Star Wars* as if it were a modern mythology is an approach that harkens back to the rhetoric around the film during its initial release. At the time, writer/director George Lucas told an interviewer, "I wanted to do a modern fairy tale, a myth" (Zito 1978:13). Film critics, journalists, and scholars picked up on George Lucas's pastiche of American popular culture (which includes everything from Disney's versions of European fairy tales, pulp science-fiction stories and serials, Westerns, and Akira Kurosawa's Japanese samurai epics) and wrote articles like Andrew Gordon's "*Star Wars:* A Myth for Our Time," in which Gordon writes: "In the absence of any shared contemporary myths, Lucas has constructed out of the usable past, out of bits of American pop culture, a new mythology which can satisfy the emotional needs of both children and adults" (1978:315).

The triumph of this point of view came in 1987 when Joseph Campbell, architect of the seminal works on mythology *The Hero with a Thousand Faces* (1949) and the four-volume *Masks of God* (1959–1968), was filmed at Lucas's own Skywalker Ranch in a series of conversations with telejournalist Bill Moyers. In these conversations, which were eventually released on PBS as the successful series *Moyers: Joseph Campbell and the Power of Myth*, Moyers seems to take every opportunity he can to ask Campbell to comment on the mythic themes in *Star Wars*. Campbell, who had never even seen the films until Lucas invited him and his wife over for a private screening of all three films (Campbell 1990:216), courteously obliged Moyers and used *Star Wars* examples when expounding upon the meaning of certain reoccurring mythic archetypes and themes: "*Star Wars* is not a simple morality play, it has to do with the powers of life as they are either fulfilled or broken and suppressed through the action of man" (Campbell 1991:145).

Exhibit curator Henderson reiterates this idea of *Star Wars* as mythology in the beautifully designed companion book to the Smithsonian exhibit. The 214-page book follows the same format as the exhibit: twenty-five mythic themes (in the exhibit there are sixteen descriptive plaques) that "reveal classical mythology themes and motifs that are woven throughout the trilogy" (1997). Each such theme is given its own subheading and then elucidated in a near word-for-word reiteration of Campbell's observations on the "monomyth," a term coined by James Joyce and adapted by Campbell in order to articulate the archetypal pattern of the heroic quest described in *The Hero with a Thousand Faces*. Themes such as the hero's "Call to Adventure," "Refusal of the Call," the "Dark Road of Trials," and the hero's journey "Into the Belly of the Beast" are first introduced and then used as analytic tools in order to reveal the structure, meaning, and themes of the three *Star Wars* movies.

There is nothing particularly novel about such an approach. Not only have critics been alluding to the mythic themes in *Star Wars* for over twenty years,* but Lucas himself has said that he deliberately set out to fabricate a fairy tale using Joseph Campbell's idea of the monomyth:

> I set out to write a children's film, and I had an idea of doing a modern fairy tale.... I started working, started doing research, started writing, and a year went by. I wrote many drafts of this work and then I stumbled across *The Hero with a Thousand Faces*.... And I said, "This is it." After reading more of Joe's books I began to understand how I could do this. When that happened to me I realized how important the contribution that Joe had made to me was. I had read these books and said, Here is a lifetime of scholarship, a life of work that is distilled down into a few books that I can read in a few months that enable me to move forward with what I am trying to do and give me focus to my work. It was a great feat and very important. It's possible that if I had not run across him I would still be writing *Star Wars* today [Campbell 1990:180].

For Mary Henderson, Andrew Gordon, and other critics, to identify where Lucas used Campbell's observations is one thing, but to proceed to claim that this pattern has "transformed *Star Wars* itself into myth," as Henderson claims (1997:7), or that the popularity of the films is *because* "of the connections the films make with the collective and personal unconscious of the viewers," as Charles Champlin suggests in *George Lucas: The Creative Impulse* (1997:96), is to obscure from whence comes the authority—"the Force"—behind *Star Wars*. The authority behind the *Star Wars* story is not a universal mythic faculty within the human psyche, it is Joseph Campbell. Campbell was like a disembodied Obi-Wan Kenobi whispering

---

*In addition to works cited in this paper, see: Roger Copeland. 1977. "When Films Quote Films, They Create a New Mythology," *The New York Times* 25 September:D1; Richard Grenier. 1980. "Celebrating Defeat," *Commentary* #70.2:58–62; Aljean Harmetz. 1983. "George Lucas: Burden of Dreams," *American Film* June:36; Anne Lancashire. 1981. "Complex Design in *The Empire Strikes Back*," *Film Criticism* #5.3 (Spring):38–52; Anne Lancashire. 1984. "Once More with Feeling," *Film Criticism* #8.2 (Winter):55–66; "Tarot and *Star Wars*," *Mythlore* #76 (Spring 1994):27–31; Todd H. Sammons. 1987. "*Return of the Jedi*: Epic Graffiti," *Science-fiction Studies* #43, v.14.3 (November:355–371; David Wyatt. 1982. "*Star Wars* and the Productions of Time," *Virginia Quarterly Review* #58:600–615; Dennis Wood. 1978. "Growing Up Among the Stars," *Literature/Film Quarterly* #6:327–341.

his esoteric teachings into the receptive ear of Lu[ke]cas, his apt pupil. Bringing Campbell in front of the television cameras to explicate the mythic themes in *Star Wars* (*his* mythic themes, the ones he universalized and identified nearly forty years before, which Lucas then used as a blueprint for the films), thereby validating the "universality" of the films, is itself a supreme sleight-of-hand trick worthy of the wizards at Industrial Light and Magic.

The phenomenal popularity of *Star Wars*, a story based on Campbell's monomyth, has been used as a vindication of the universality of Campbell's work; the truth, however, is less mysterious and seductive. *Star Wars* is an exciting spectacle movie, thoughtfully conceived, well crafted, and featuring astonishing special effects thanks to innovations like the Dykstraflex Camera and the Electronic Motion Control System, which, when used in concert with the creations of the film's crack model-building team, achieved the convincing illusion of immersing the audience in another world.

Like the blockbuster *Jaws* (1975) two years previous, *Star Wars* was released at a time when the audience demographic was ideally suited for the mass appeal of a film like *Star Wars*. Created by baby boomers as their version of the ultimate child's space fantasy — the perfection of what films like the *Flash Gordon* series (1936–1940) and *Forbidden Planet* (1956) promised them in their childhood — *Star Wars* was eminently appealing to the new generation of parents (the largest number of new parents ever in America's history), who could think of nothing better to entertain their children with than that which had once entertained them.

As for those parents — the twenty- to thirty-something boomers — *Star Wars* was a palliative on many levels. By 1977 the hippie youth movement had failed to meet its own meteoric expectations throughout the cultural and political field of Cold War America. The Vietnam War had dragged on into the 1970s and had only come to a dissatisfying conclusion at the very time when Nixon was being driven from office in disgrace. The hopes many staked on rock and roll as a rallying point were dashed as Woodstock faded into the nightmare at Altamont Speedway (as shown in the concert movie *Gimme Shelter*, which, coincidentally enough, George Lucas was a cameraman for) as well as the premature deaths of many of that movement's heroes (Jimmie Hendrix, 1970; Janis Joplin, 1970; and Jim Morrison, 1971). The United States, still in the midst of the never-ending Cold War, suffered economic recession due to two oil shocks during the 1970s. Families and neighborhoods were affected as businesses closed or relocated, more often than not out of the city and into the suburbs. All this left many Americans exasperated and exhausted as their security, pride, and hope for the future were threatened.

Star Wars made people feel better. It gave them an opportunity to celebrate victory through a clear and unambiguous polarization of moral and political forces (the good and the bad) to which the 1977-dominant baby boom generation had been conditioned to respond (the 1950s Red scare, cowboy and Indian serials on the Saturday-afternoon matinee screen, Matt Dillon and *The Lone Ranger* cantering through black-and-white pixelated Dodge Cities, Tombstones, Amarillos, and other desert prairie towns as vacant and relaxed as the newborn American suburb). The unambiguous contexts in which the baby boomers were raised were frustrated and complicated during the 1960s and 1970s. They were, however, joyfully reaffirmed (in fantasy if not in fact) through *Star Wars* and its contemporary forms of fantasy participation: everything from the punk relocation back to a 1950s-styled arena of contest (us and them, "never mind those bollucks"), a *Dungeons & Dragons* form of role-playing game morality in which "lawful good" characters slay "chaotic evil" orcs, and professional wrestling, wherein the production of comfortable dichotomies takes the form of Hulk Hogan vs. The Iron Sheik.

Robert G. Collins, in "*Star Wars*: The Pastiche of Myth and the Yearning for a Past Future," may choose to gloss over this demographic foundation for *Star Wars*' force in America's collective psyche, asserting instead that "*Star Wars* confronts us as the first omnibus work of generalized myth in the film medium" (1977:2), but what he and writers of his ilk have failed to grasp, and what Campbell himself observes, is that there is no "generalized myth." All mythology is grounded in the particulars of a society and culture, in a people's way of life, in the *praxis*—the practice—of living in a specific time and place.

Nevertheless, Henderson's *Star Wars: The Magic of Myth* may not be misguided in its effort to identify Arthurian, Christian, Zen Buddhist, and whatever other mythological themes, archetypes, or tropes are to be found in *Star Wars*. Of course, the themes are going to be there because Lucas deliberately drew from this material in writing *Star Wars*! A work like Henderson's can, therefore, prove useful in gaining a deeper appreciation for Lucas's deliberate attempt to appropriate patterns and themes from Campbell's observations (which stress the similarity—universality?—of mythic themes by citing specific ritual practices or stories when they correspond to his idea of the monomyth). At the Smithsonian exhibit, it is interesting to read the exhibit plaque that explains how the mythological "Belly of the Beast" motif (drawn from *The Hero with a Thousand Faces*) is used as the setting for transformative events in the lives of the characters in *The Empire Strikes Back*. The plaque notes that Darth Vader only begins to show his weakness and eventual fallibility once he emerges from his cocoon-like meditation chamber. Vader does this first through appearing unhelmeted for a brief moment, so that we see his bald, scarred, old-man's head, and second, through immediately leaving his chamber and bowing before the Emperor, revealing for the first time that Vader is a servant to a higher master. Similarly, it is in the belly of the giant space slug that Han and Leia's romance finally blossoms into a kiss. Finally, it is in the dank, womblike swamp cave of the planet Dagobah where Luke confronts a vision of Darth Vader as a dark shadow of himself. These observations can enrich one's appreciation of the film. However, it can hardly be used as evidence that such a mythic theme is universal simply because *Star Wars* used it. Nor does it move *Star Wars* itself any closer to being a myth. Observations that suggest *Star Wars* and its artifacts have achieved the status of mythology are misguided. Even more than that, they malign the idea of mythology and its relevance for a community of people. The message of *Star Wars*, when viewed in the context of the society from which it comes, is that of a modern-day anti-myth.

In *Masks of God* (a work referred to much less often than *Hero with a Thousand Faces*, but a work that nevertheless represents the author at the height of his literary powers), Campbell identifies four functions of mythology. The first function is to instill within the person a sense of awe and beauty at the magnitude, wonder, and plurality (both physical and spiritual) of the universe. The second function is to explain why the world is the way it is: why the sky is blue, why snakes do not have legs, and so forth (such stories are called etiologic tales)— it establishes the cosmology of the world for a people. The third function teaches people how to live a model life despite all manner of circumstances— it enforces a moral order. Finally, the fourth function of mythology, what Campbell identifies as its most important, "is to foster the centering and unfolding of the individual in integrity, in accord with" oneself, one's culture, the universe, and the "awesome ultimate mystery which is both beyond himself and all things" (1968:4–6). Campbell generally asserted that, in our society, science has picked up the explanation of the cosmos (the second function); art, the awe and beauty of the universe, as well as the instilling of a moral order (the first and third functions); and that, in the wake of the collapse of our ancestral mythology, nothing has yet stepped in to satisfy the fourth function — how one lives in accord with the rest of the universe — which is bound up with ritual: therefore we get random acts of violence, surreptitious gang activities, and other evidences of an unbridled, chaotic world filled with unbridled, chaotic men and women (Campbell 1991:82).

The experience of watching *Star Wars* is an experience of an overwhelming "imaginary." The famous opening shot of *Star Wars*, in which an Imperial Star Destroyer cruises over the audience's head, exhausts one even before the story begins. Richard Edlund knew that shot would determine how audiences would respond to the film's subsequent special effects. It is the longest special effects shot in the film, and it was shot five times until Edlund was certain that he had it right. The shot lures the viewer into the imaginary world of the film. The Smithsonian exhibit and accompanying book try to configure the three films' six hours of the imaginary into the sphere of the symbolic. They do this through language — a necessity for symbolic systems — such as the sixteen plaques spaced throughout the exhibit, which recontextualize the artifacts from the film into a symbolic code Campbell derived from his study of the world's mythology (primarily Hindu, Buddhist, Christian, Islamic, American Indian, Egyptian, prehistorical shamanism, and Zoroastrian religions), artists (Arthurian poets, Richard Wagner, Walt Whitman, T. S. Eliot, Robinson Jeffers, Pablo Picasso, Thomas Mann, and, especially, James Joyce), and philosophers (Immanuel Kant, Arthur Schopenhauer, Friedrich Nietzsche, Sigmund Freud, Carl Jung, D. T. Suzuki, Mircea Eliade, and Martin Buber).

This endeavor, while not arbitrary, is misguided in that it attempts — using Campbell as a kind of superego father figure — to structure the audience's experience of the imaginary in the film into a symbolic code. They use the term "mythology" for this symbolic order. However, from a look at how Campbell's four functions of mythology are fulfilled in America today it is clear that society's efficacious mythology is not the story of the movement of heroic archetypes through a liminal field, as Campbell identifies in the foundational text of the exhibit, *The Hero with a Thousand Faces*. Rather, our contemporary mythology is the story of the manufacture of the "individual" from recombined bits of archived information (Critical Art Ensemble 1994). Our mythology is the electronic archiving of quantified individuality according to scientific methods, and an implementation of this process in order to serve the capitalism upon which our economy is based. "Our atrocity," writes Baudrillard, "is exactly inverse of that of the former centuries. It is to efface blood and cruelty by objectivity" (1983:1).

A pioneering work in the field of ethnography, Arnold Van Gennep's *Rites of Passage* (1908), upon which Campbell based many of his observations, identified a three-phase sequence of events during mythological rituals (Campbell's fourth function of mythology could be called the ritual function):

Separation from the Community→
Liminal Stage→
Reincorporation into the Community

When watching a movie, the viewer is separated from his community, displaced in a darkened theater. For the two-hour duration of the film, the audience is in a liminal state, inhabiting the imaginary. Performance studies theorist Richard Schechner might call this state one of double negativity: the viewer is both *not there* in the theater (for he or she is lost in the image) and *not not there* in the theater (for surely a body sits in the darkened room) (1985:123).

However, with *Star Wars*, Van Gennep's third stage is never achieved. When the last credits roll, John Williams's score ceases, and the lights go on, the viewer returns to the community, but he or she is not reincorporated into the community after such a liminal experience. The liminal experience of the film has no avenue into which it can be reincorporated into *praxis*—daily experience. *Star Wars*–as–image fails in an essential mythological function: it can take you "out there," but it cannot take you back. And, in taking the viewer "out there" to a galaxy far, far away, it is really doing nothing more than stranding the audience in a liminal stage in which they are excluded from the larger non–*Star Wars* community. The film is a two-hour liminal experience that excites the passions and nerves of the audience. Leaving the theater all worked up but with no obvious direction in which to apply (reincorporate) this energy, the viewer may quell this tension by returning to the queue wrapped around the theater in order to watch it again. What other way is there of doing something with this experience of having watched the film? Its life as video or DVD is guaranteed — the *form* guarantees a successful market performance. So the viewer returns to the theater line or video store or the Smithsonian National Air and Space Museum. Here, inside the museum that deigns to honor scientific man's most lauded achievements in air and space exploration, the *Star Wars* phenomenon plays into the scientific rhetoric and capitalist ideology that shapes our contemporary mythology. Though it does so with mythological motifs that Henderson, Gordon, Collins, and Champlin may not suspect.

Star Wars cannot reincorporate its viewers back into the community with an impartation any kind of efficacious knowledge, as the mythological rites of passage that Van Gennep writes about do, because the experience of watching *Star Wars* is not corporeal — it is imaginary, a body (as French philosophers Deleuze and Guattari would say) without organs. The Critical Art Ensemble observes that "If the BwO [Body without Organs] is conceived of as appearance of self contained in screenal space, it is nearly supernatural to think that the BwO can possess the flesh and walk the earth" (1994:7–8). This near-supernatural process is a moment of possible weakness, they continue, because it subjects the imaginary to the limits of the real, but it is also a moment of amplification for the spectacle. The *Star Wars* exhibition is an example of the celebrity of objecthood. During the press conference before the event's unveiling, it was announced that Chewbacca, R2-D2, C-3PO, and Darth Vader were in the exhibit, and that George Lucas would be conducting interviews "next to Chewbacca." In a film in which masks and costumes very often *are* the characters, the public display of the costumes is equivalent to the "flesh possession" of the spectacle of the image.

Marshall Blonsky relates that Malraux identified the function of museums as ripping the work from the "setting of its age," and the museologist "must institutionalize the rip-away" (1996:2). Henderson and her associates have ripped the elements of *Star Wars* from their imaginary context, have displayed them to the public, hungry for the "assurances of the pre-electronic order," and have, in so doing, both strengthened the spectacle of the film itself by presenting its elements apart from the spectacle, thereby amplifying the value of that spectacle, and written a symbolic code to contextualize the *Star Wars* image, institutionalizing that symbolic code through its public presentation in the National Air and Space Museum, and, having done so, introduced an ideological subtext into a nostalgic process (and even pilgrimage) for two generations: the baby boomers and their children.

Establishing an exhibition of the artifacts of a film would, merely by its intent, be an example of the Critical Art Ensemble's physical avatar of the electronic world. However, by ordering the exhibition according to a symbolic code — the monomyth of Campbell — the Smithsonian exhibit determines the context in which two generations of viewers experience the physical avatar — the celebrityhood — of the film. In the *Star Wars* exhibit the "nearly supernatural" Body without Organs has been incarnated in the flesh and made to "walk the earth," or at least the National Air and Space Museum's second floor. The pervading sense that something is lost or hidden within the subtext of *Star Wars* is what sustains the exhibit, which purports to reveal the hidden mythological underpinnings of the film. The audience's desire to rediscover itself in the image of the film compels the viewer to become a pilgrim, to travel to the exhibit, where the fading image of the film is both recontextualized into a symbolic code and is finally reified from out of the electronic ether of the imaginary. Part of the film is materialized, but at the same time, what is not materialized — the experience of watching the film (complete with John Williams's score) — is made that much more untouchable.

The exhibit, trying to promote the idea that *Star Wars* is a mythology, is engaging in an ideological attempt to change the phenomenological experience of the film. Through an attribution of *Star Wars* as mythology, the Smithsonian is attempting to raise its cultural worth and importance. They are, of course, obligated to do this because their reason for creating a *Star Wars* exhibit — to exploit its extraordinary popularity in order to increase the museum's revenue — would never fly as the sole means of justifying the inclusion of artifacts from a space fantasy movie in a museum devoted to humankind's real efforts to explore space. Therefore, they must increase the cultural worth of their object before they use that object (as a sort of Hope Diamond on display behind museum glass) to increase their economic worth.

The message and themes of *Star Wars* are decidedly nonscientific: the story tells us to follow our hearts, to rely on intuition and not technological devices. The story tells us not to rely on technology to save us, that, in fact, we *cannot* rely on technology to save us. Yet the films require the latest technological advances in sound and picture-recording technology in order to be told: George Lucas waited twelve years before beginning his new trilogy of *Star Wars* prequels, waiting for computer imaging technology to catch up with his imagination!

The *Star Wars* message is, in fact, an anti-mythological message, precisely because its message about the human spirit is assembled from the remnants of the old mythologies— mythologies that no longer carry weight in the way we live our lives today— and runs perpendicular to the scientific capitalism mythology of our day. The *Star Wars* films are an anti-mythological message contained within a form — the films— that is very much a product of our contemporary— scientific and capitalist — mythology. How appropriate, then, that the Smithsonian has chosen to exhibit the anti-mythological artifacts of the films inside its temple to the real mythological artifacts of our day: the airplanes, rockets, and space stations of scientists reaching to walk the sky and sail the stars. In the exhibit "*Star Wars*: The Magic of Myth," as in the films, an anti-mythological message is contained inside a very contemporary mythological format. That *Star Wars* does this in a form so palatable to our way of seeing and living perhaps makes that pill a little easier to swallow. Let us just hope that its form does not anesthetize us to its, thankfully, anti-mythological themes.

Man and Myth:
Social Implications
of Chris Carter and
The X-Files

BY JENNIFER ANDERSON

On Sunday evenings, nationwide, twenty million people stop whatever they are doing and sit for one sacred hour in front of the television. They stop their otherwise normal lives to immerse themselves into *The X-Files*. Fox Mulder, a believer in the paranormal, and Dana Scully, a believer in science, are two FBI agents. They take us on adventures across the country and around the world as they seek to find the truth that lies in *The X-Files*. *The X-Files* are a series of unexplained cases that were ignored by the FBI, and would have remained lost forever had Mulder not lobbied to have them opened. After undergoing hypnotherapy, he recovered the memory that his little sister, Samantha, was abducted by aliens. He has dedicated his life to finding her and subsequently begun uncovering all the dirty little secrets of the government. In his investigations, he has uncovered a series of plots by the American government against the American people. Because he started to ask the right questions, the "powers that be" got nervous. They assigned Scully as his partner to use her medical knowledge to debunk his missions. What has followed is a dichotomy between friendship and partnership.

The show was created by Chris Carter, former editor of *Surfing Magazine* and now a screenwriter. He shopped the idea around to FOX, of creating a show that is scary, new, and does something that is not currently available on television. He wanted to make an intelligent, sexy, eerie show that would appeal to all walks of life regardless of religion, education, or common sense. What he has succeeded in creating is a universe in which our government is in alliance with other powerful men around the world in a giant conspiracy to form a new world power with an alien race that settled on this planet centuries ago. And by creating this alternate universe on television, he has amassed a following of fans who want to believe in the theories, myths, and stories they are "fed" every week. Having amassed this following, he has created a myth that is followed almost in the same manner as one follows religion. In the recent movie *Can't Hardly Wait*, two social pariahs of a graduating high school class wear the show's most famous two logos on their shirts: *Trust No One* and *The Truth is Out There*. Moreover, the rock band Eve 6 took their name from a character on the show. Thus, Carter has taken an idea and turned his fantasy into a mul-timillion-dollar enterprise. However, I believe that he subscribes neither to the myth he promotes nor the cult it has created.

With the creation of *The X-Files*, Carter has made the government the bad guys, aliens real, and science inadequate nine times out of ten. Every fan of the show now finds it possible to think Big Brother may really be watching our every move, and instead of backing off, Carter goes further with every episode. *The X-Files* have become his "social front." Fans want to know about the man behind the myth. They clamor to read interviews and hear what he has to say in order to get an idea of whether the man behind the show really believes any of his press. Some believe he subscribes to the whole story from beginning to end, while others think he is just try-ing to create a fantasy world that sells well and is entertaining in the process. By looking at the way Carter portrays himself and his show, I plan to show how his myth is perpetuated in popular culture with the exam-ples of a website and a fan magazine. I will conclude with an attempt to uncover the truth about this clandestine man and his real opinion on the myth he has created.

Everything begins with the imaginary entertainment environment, an idea borrowed for our purposes from the work of Daniel Mackay. This is the fantasy world of events. "The imaginary entertainment environ-ment is, instead, regarded as a place for play — for nonproductivity — with no use value in relation to the architecture of everyday life" (2001:145). In this instance, it is the world in which *The X-Files* take place. It is a world similar to the world we really live in, but there are elements of the fan-tastic that keep it imaginary. This overlaps into the drama. Schechner defines *drama* as "a written text, score scenario, instruction, plan or map. The drama can be taken from place to place or from time to time independent of the person or people who carry it. These people may be just 'messengers', even unable to read the drama, no less comprehend or enact it" (1988:72). The story line of *The X-Files* is about two FBI special agents out to prove or disprove using science and guttural belief that the paranormal occurrences they encounter are in fact paranormal. Mulder is the believer who wants all the things he sees to be true, and Scully is the skeptic who wants all that she sees to have scientific verification. Together they set out week after week to find the truly strange and either prove or disprove its existence. Carter uses these characters and this basic framework to help perpetuate his myth.

The script for *The X-Files* is television and cinema. "Script: all that can be transmitted from time to time and place to place; the basic code of the events. The script is transmitted person to person, the transmitter is not a mere messenger. The transmitter of the script must know the script and be able to teach it to others. This teaching may be conscious or through empathetic, emphatic means" (Schechner 1988:72). In the beginning, the imaginary entertainment environment and the drama were brought into the homes of millions every week through television. All one had to do was sit and tune in to this imaginary world, and for an hour it seemed as real as the world in which we live. Now, Carter has broadened his own script by taking his drama into movie theaters. The faithful who tune in every week can see their heroes enlarged on a big screen, and those who may not have been fans may find themselves drawn into the dark and mysterious world of *The X-Files* due in part to the ambiance of the movies. What more appropriate place to delve into the horrors of alien invasion and governmental experimentation than in a movie theater?

Theater is "the event enacted by a specific group of performers; what the performers actually do during the production. The theater is concrete and immediate. Usually the theater is a manifestation or representation of the drama and/or script" (Schechner 1988:72). We only get to see the theories and conspiracies that Carter wants us to see. He shows us the drama he wants us to see and hopes we will believe and follow him along his path. We see only enough of the behind-the-scenes workings of the government to keep us intrigued, and usually just enough to make us tune in the next week to see more. And this leads to the performance. "Performance: The whole constellation of events, most of them passing unnoticed, that take place in/among both performers and audience from the time the first spectator enters the field of the performance — the precinct where the theater takes place — to the time the last spectator leaves" (72). By enticing us to watch week after week, *The X-Files* have become part of our society. Even those who do not watch the show are familiar enough with the characters that they can tune in once in a while and not be too confused. However, those who do watch faithfully are educated enough on the history of the show and its characters that every bit of information opens the doors to more questions. As a result, web pages, card games, novels, and role-playing games have developed as a way to help the fans answer their own questions and create more. The ancillary *X-Files* sites become a further performance of the show.

On December 7, 1998, at 2:26 P.M., I logged onto *The X-Files* webpage created by a fan named Asher (this page is found at *www.geocities.com*). As a performance, this site is made up of its own unique form. The script, in this case, is composed of the various elements used on the web: images, scroll bars, frames, and so forth. As the user clicks on these various functions and moves through the site, the performance is enacted: the screen becomes a digital stage where the participant performs in the imaginary entertainment environment of *The X-Files*. A prompt box appears before the page is finished loading, and it asks for an identity. It then tells the user how many people have visited the sight, at that point there were 28,479 visitors. The background is black, and the logo of *The X-Files* is scrawled across the screen one and a half times. The rectangular black box at the top of the screen has a large Asher's "X-Files Page" that shrinks and moves up to the left side of the screen. Then the words "Pic's," "Sounds," "Movies," with "Chat" appear, the first three stacked on top of each other in that order, with "Chat" all alone. The words "And More" are written sideways next to it.

As a participant, the user shares in the performance of *The X-Files* myth, and consequently this website is full of tropes from *The X-Files*, including the fact that this page is set on a dark background, expressing the similar trope that there is hardly ever a light and bright episode of the show. In addition, Asher incorporates sounds to make his page complete — similar to Carter, who felt the show was lacking in completion, and created, with the help of the music world, two sound tracks to the show and one to the movie. By putting all this information out on the World Wide Web, Asher has made it accessible to anyone with a computer. He has made an environment in which his friends and fellow fans can interact through chat rooms, e-mail addresses, and other webpages. This site includes a scrolling bar on the left, with pictures of Scully, Mulder, and *The X-Files* logo, each with links, in blue, taking the user to picture locations, an episode guide, a chat room, sound bites, and a site about the film. For example, users clicking on the "Other Pics" link on the lefthand scroll bar area taken to another location, presumably still Asher's, that states, "Here are *X-Files* Pictures" in bold, red letters. Slowly, the blue outlined boxes begin to reveal thirty-one pictures of characters on the show. This sort of fan enthusiasm has opened the door for new kinds of media involvement by people who do not have access to the money and power of Hollywood producers. Here, fan web designers get to perform the role of a creative producer, borrowing content from a television show they love and creating a digital stage where they can perform their own "X-Philes" (as fans are called) desire in a public forum to be shared with a computer-literate audience.

Another medium through which Carter gets his myth perpetuated is *The X-Files Official Magazine.* Here, Carter can make sure that only the information he wants to be made known will be made available. It gives him more control over the media availability of the show. Also, the fans will be more likely to buy a magazine that has his stamp of approval because it gives the impression that they are getting the truth as Carter sees it. At the same time, it leaves enough room for the audience to participate by including them in articles and columns being written, enabling them to keep informed about the workings of the set, announcing the new merchandise being made available, and notifying them of upcoming events of the season.

The cover to one example of this magazine is made from glossy paper that almost slides out of the reader's hands and has an expensive, official appearance. It contains a picture of the two lead characters on the front and the titles of the four main articles on the left, with a "bonus-behind-the-scenes of the new set" announcement across the front. The kinds of information that the reader can find inside include an editorial that takes the devil's advocate approach to whether Mulder and Scully should end their platonic relationship and become intimate. Apparently, this query was put forth to the readers and the majority replied that they should finally become lovers. And, as a further incentive to keep this discussion going, the magazine includes a ballot box inviting the X-Philes to again cast their votes about whether Mulder and Scully should become lovers. In addition, the magazine contains feature articles, such as one about Mitch Pileggi, the former boss of Mulder and Scully, an "insiders peek" into Mulder's apartment, as well as interviews with cast and crew members. There is also an advertisement for a replica of the alien in the movie. The only legitimate feature article in the magazine is about the Behavioral Science division of the FBI. Such magazines allow fans to get a "behind-the-scenes" look at their favorite media shows, placing them into an immersive fantasy environment where what they previously viewed on television and on film gets slowed down, materialized as a thing they can hold in their hands. The producers, in effect, offer a different kind of performance: one that "invites" fans backstage and takes them on a tour, seemingly privileging them as "guests," and ensuring that fan interest in the show remains high.

Chris Carter has tapped into the existing cultural codes in American society by basing his show on science and the scientific method. Because of this, people are able to seemingly follow logically the path the show leads them down. It becomes unimportant whether what he says can really happen, but rather how well it will be scientifically explained. Also, Carter created *The X-Files* to realize his fascination with the supernatural. He had a desire to put something on television that had never been done before. He wanted to create something scary that would still be intellectual enough to sustain the intelligentsia, yet accessible to the common viewer. He takes great pains to ensure that the science is irrefutable and that the creativity is unmatched. Using the national fear of alien abductions, governmental conspiracies, and the boogie monster, he has manipulated the world into believing that what he puts out there on some level — even if it is just for one hour on Sunday evenings — is possible. But does Chris Carter believe everything he puts his name on? Does he sit up at night waiting for aliens to land in his backyard, and does he think the government had a secret cure for cancer, or does he just find it all to be intriguing fiction that has amassed a small fortune for him? The truth is out there!

Alex Proyas:
A Consistent Image

BY CLAUDIA DEBS

A native of Egypt, Alex Proyas moved to Australia at the age of three and entered film school by the age of seventeen. After graduation, he and other students began their own film company, working mostly on music videos. This enabled Proyas to make a move to Los Angeles and begin his career. He came to be well known for his work on commercials and for MTV music videos, which some critics have claimed reveals itself too much in his feature films, arguing that many of the images in his films are shot too quickly when they should be sustained for a longer period of time. Proyas directed *The Crow* (1994) which has already been tagged a cult classic. Based on a comic book, *The Crow* was a tragic love story that addressed the darker sides of vengeance and life after death. He also wrote, directed, and produced *Dark City* (1998), which has been both praised and bludgeoned, but always prefaced with his ever-present gothic science-fiction approach.

In his films, specifically *The Crow* and *Dark City*, Proyas perpetuates a symbolic representation of his own perceptions of life, as well as the most extreme possibilities of what life may be. Stylistically, he uses the gothic, "noir," and science-fiction genres to convey his ideas. The recurring themes of Proyas can be analyzed in order to show how they are consistent with the images created in his films. Around these images the overall mystique of Alex Proyas is created. Furthermore, after dissecting the aforementioned films, a semiotic examination of webpages, magazines, and interviews will reveal how this mystique is perpetuated in these forms. As a result, these images and the manifestation of these images are constantly being bled into one another, essentially re-performing themselves in a symbiotic relationship. The primary basis for the world that Alex Proyas creates for his films is that of an enigmatic environment, somewhere between that of a surrealist and an expressionist one.

Upon achieving the status of a feature film director, Proyas was already marked with an incident of death. This image, whether he liked it or not, became an iconic mark indelibly placed on Proyas's "social front" (Goffman 1959). At the end of the filming of *The Crow,* Brandon Lee was killed on the set. This image overshadowed the movie, raising the intrigue that the movie incites. When seeing the movie, people wondered which scene Lee was actually killed in and whether that scene was cut. When questions were not being answered by the film production company, Proyas's image as a death-tainted director was created and became performed in popular culture. It is this role that persisted in Proyas's next movie, as well as in interviews, magazines, and websites. Moreover, the fact that *The Crow* was a story based on a graphic-novel character caused any future endeavors of the graphic-story series to be tainted by Proyas's adaptation of it.

In his next film, using the same style of setting and dark imagery, Proyas created an imaginary world that far surpassed that of *The Crow.* In *Dark City,* he was now the writer, director, and producer. It was this film that fully embodied Proyas's philosophical beliefs, and as a result continued to sculpt his popular image. In film reviews, *Dark City* has been labeled "a visually stunning, Kafka-esque creation with minor imperfections" (Dyer 1998). Less admiring critics argued that the images in the movie were much too fleeting, very much like an MTV music video. They attributed this style to Proyas's previous work with music videos and commercials. In all of the film reviews of *Dark City,* however, one thing was constant, and that was the underlying thematic concept of the film and its relation to the director and his previous film.

Alex Proyas's image is re-performed in society by film critics and fans and through websites. The image he has obtained is that of a man of dark mystery who addresses humankind's issues through the science-fiction and fantasy genres. Although not all critics support his work, their analysis of his films, whether intentional or not, are always in agreement, proving that Proyas has a decisive technique with which he gets his point across. He intelligently uses universal questions as the core of his works. As a genre, science-fiction extrapolates on certain facts and stretches them into something that may be conceivable. Fantasy, on the other hand, operates on notions of impossibility. What Proyas does is to create a world in which the two coalesce. In *The Crow,* the world is as we know it; the emotions that the characters endure are real, human emotions. The characters are identifiable by an audience, and the events that happen are feasible up to a point. However, fantasy comes to the forefront when the soul of the protagonist (Eric Draven) comes back from the dead in his corporeal body to avenge the brutal killing of himself and his fiancée with special powers that are shared by a crow. The motivation for this vengeance may be real, but its manifestation is through fantasy.

Dark City is more profound in its confrontation with universal issues. In this sense, this movie teeters more toward the science-fiction genre, but skillfully combined with fantasy. Its major points are the questions that have existed for ages: Who are we? Where do we come from? Are we the only beings in the universe? Who is in control of this universe? What is our place in the universe? What makes us human? One way in which he addresses these questions is through memory. The story operates on the premise that memory is what makes us human, because so much of our memory is connected to emotion. Yet memory can be dangerously manipulated, as it is in the film. The main character, John Murdoch, awakes in a hotel bathtub without any memory of who he is or how he got there. As the story unfolds, the audience learns, along with the characters, that our memories are influenced by many things (in the movie they are subject to the Strangers, a dying alien race) and that they are unreliable. Through this approach, Proyas blurs the distinction between reality and unreality.

The subconscious is brought to the fore while everything is in question. The Strangers are able to alter physical realities and to control the city by making humans fall asleep on command. In search for a cure for their dying species, they look to humans to seek out what it is that makes them human. They think it is the human soul that separates them, and that the way to the soul is through the memories that are linked to human emotion. As Roger Luckhurst states, "this is another SF trope: alien technological superiority comes with the loss of vitality of emotion" (1998:39). Murdoch is unable to discern which of his memories are real and which are not. The way Proyas uses these issues in his own work is also supported by Luckhurst's statement that "alien abduction is a surprising confirmation of the argument Istvan Csicery-Ronay, Jr., has made that 'SF has ceased to be a genre of fiction *per se,* becoming instead a mode of awareness about the world'" (29). In *Dark City* it is never clear that the humans under the Strangers' influence were taken from Earth, nor is it specified where they are in the universe. These questions are never resolved, and the past, present, and future are not definite. Thus, the world of the characters is never known.

All of these mystical references to the unknown are present in the performance of Alex Proyas in popular culture, as well. Part of what establishes this image is the way he is portrayed by film critics, fans, and also by himself. In every review of either of the two movies, reference is given to Proyas's forte for creating highly aesthetic visuals that mesmerize. Some claim that he pays more attention to visuals than to the content of the movie. Nonetheless, he is very often likened to such directors as Ridley Scott (*Blade Runner*) and Stanley Kubrick. These references to established directors gives Proyas a sort of credibility that is equivalent to "the truth." The truth here is that Proyas becomes credible when his style is compared to those who have already established their credibility. These comparisons were first made after *The Crow*, and Proyas fulfills his role (which was created by popular culture) further in *Dark City*. The names Kubrick and Scott carry within them a sociocultural code. Within this code is a social reality, that of the reputation of these directors. Because of this, Proyas's name in the film world has taken on a metalinguistic code. His name now becomes a double meaning: he becomes the director whose style is just as good as other directors known around the world. However, this image is manipulated further by critics and fans because after making such a comparison, it is argued at times that he has a distinct style that cannot be mistaken for anyone else's. Therefore, it can be inferred: Alex Proyas is a director whose end products are visually stunning, thought-oriented works of science fiction and fantasy that embody the expertise of directors such as Kubrick and Scott. Furthermore, Proyas has surpassed them in that he has developed a distinct style and name for himself through his work such that his films are consistent in their portrayal of the environments in which they take place.

Next in my analysis of the image of Alex Proyas is the study of a *Dark City* webpage. Webpages have become another realm where the world of a movie and the image of its director are re-performed by "restoring behavior" (as Schechner would say) from the movie as a reference. "Restored behavior is used in all kinds of performances," Schechner notes (1985:35). These "strips of behavior" are the background established by the director, Alex Proyas. In the movie's official webpage (*www.darkcity.com*), perhaps the first most striking element of its construction is its completely black background. In conjunction with the feel of the movie, the webpage suggests mystery, the existence of something innate within what is seen firsthand; or rather, in treating the introductory page as the first "lexia," the colors are codified with significance, as Barthes might say (1985:85). The colors used are black and gray, dark colors that contain within themselves a sociocultural code linked to death, mourning, evil, and the otherworldly. As in *The Crow*, *Dark City* has a gothic, expressionistic style that uses somber colors and the absence of light to create the essence of the imaginary film environment.

The webpage continues as a performance of the movie and, of course, as Proyas himself. On the top center of the first lexia, the words DARK CITY, all in capital letters, flash on and off. They go from jumbled, nonsensical symbols back to the words DARK CITY, immediately grabbing attention as they blink rhythmically and methodically on the screen. This blinking calls the viewer's attention to these words, placing an unknown importance on them. Directly beneath is the phrase YOU ARE NOT WHO YOU THINK YOU ARE, which blinks in the same fashion. The blinking words correspond directly to Murdoch's pursuit in finding what memories are real and which are fabricated, or not his own. This is what Barthes would refer to as the positioning of the enigma (1985:87): implying that there is a truth to be known, which, in this case, would only be found through exploring the webpage. To the left of this, in the same presentation, the word TUNE appears also in gray letters. Directly beneath that word are the blinking words CHANGE YOUR REALITY. This is simply a trope (or strip of behavior) of the movie itself used to maintain consistency with the movie. "Tuning" is what the Strangers call their ability to change physical realities, stop time, and manipulate the citizens of the city. The inhabitants of the city are completely unaware that this happens. Therefore, each time the Strangers tune, every person's reality is changed, using memory injection. This leads to the next part of the page just below the word TUNE. Beneath it are the words MEMORY INJECTION, which also flash on and off, and below it are the words CHANGE ANOTHER PERSON'S REALITY. To the right of that are the words WAKE UP, and below that is the phrase MOVIE FACTS. Finally, at the very bottom of the page is the word ESCAPE, and underneath that the phrase A GAME. The phrases beneath the words are not only explanations of what the words mean; their presence suggests that there are two truths to be known. They suggest two realities that have a doubled meaning, in a metalinguistic way. The person viewing the site is thrown into this world, which is perfectly congruent with the film. It is as if the set designers of the film also designed the webpage.

Perhaps the most eccentric part of this webpage is the music that accompanies it. It is somber, heavy, and brooding. It plays continuously until one "clicks" to another page of the website. Even for those who visit the site who have not seen the movie, the feeling that there is a truth to be found is strategically placed as the basis of the site. At the very bottom of the page is a link that says: Chat Live with Alex Proyas. Unfortunately, one finds that the live chat happened before the movie was released on

February 26, 1998, but the conversation from it is printed in interview form. Most of the other links are just images from the film itself, mostly filled with dark colors: blacks browns, grays, and occasionally deep reds, which imbue the image of the movie and its director with the film noir style for which Proyas is known. It is rather interesting that most people know Proyas's work, yet they still do not know his name. In one way, this may be considered an insult. On the other hand, however, in speaking of his reputation, he is consistently recognized as creating visually arresting and cleverly stylized films. This image is supported in film reviews especially, but the live chat interview is perhaps the first doorway to the mind of Proyas's point of view.

In the live chat, Proyas willingly supports his presentation of himself in society. His work is what set the fundamental structure of the image, and through fan reaction, websites, film reviews, and particularly the live chat, Proyas himself, his fans, and his co-workers all agree with his image of eccentricity. Although his uniqueness is manifested in his films, people who have worked with him present an image of someone who immerses himself in his work but at the same time is very approachable. In the live chat, the set designer, Patrick Tatopoulos claims that his and Proyas's visual ideas never faced conflict. Whether this is true or not, it creates another dimension of Proyas's image as a director. Proyas confirms this by saying that they were always "both together." This sense of collaboration on all the aspects of the film, whether it was with the set designers, scriptwriters, or actors, is followed throughout the entire chat.

Tatopoulos further states that "the world was really created by Alex, I just helped paint it." This statement implies that Proyas is the sole genius behind the masterpiece. Tatopoulos furthers this image by portraying Proyas as a very down-to-earth type of man who is capable of more than the average person, saying that "he brought inspiration." It may seem that both Tatopoulos and Proyas are both being overly modest, for every time Tatopoulos praises Proyas's genius, Proyas responds that "Patrick is being very humble. He set up the whole tone of the movie ... and Patrick would come back with these drawings that not only inspired the studios but inspired the writing process."

It is also very clear that the concept of the film originated with Proyas, who, states in the live chat: "The paranoid aspect of the story came out of dreams I had as a child — that while I was asleep, dark figures would come into my bedroom and rearrange things. Maybe the way I envisioned it was a bit bizarre, but I think being afraid of the dark is a very basic childhood fear. Whenever I would come across that concept as a kid, it would haunt me and make me re-examine the way I looked at things." This statement also encompasses the fear of the lead character, Murdoch, throughout the film. He is a paranoid character in constant question of reality, and rightly so, because there really are dark figures rearranging things. This typifies how Proyas's images are portrayed consistently through his work.

Although not every movie critic likes Proyas's work, almost all of them give the same commentary: that he uses film noir, gothic, and science-fiction genres to convey his own personal and intellectual fears of paranoia and the search for a truth that goes beyond conventional realism. They say that he completely throws himself into his work concerning every detail, from music to set design and character delineation. "Being a film director in this day and age is predominantly about that conflict," Proyas says. "I don't think you have to 'sell out,' but you need to have some responsibility to the people who invest in your movie. It's not that they can't be works of art, but the challenge is to make the best movie you can make" (*www.darkcity.com*). In doing so, he has established a reputation, and along with his own presentation of self being compared to such directing superstars as Stanley Kubrick and even Fritz Lang, he is given an authentic credibility.

A Robert Jordan
Book Signing

BY JESSE SNEDDEN

In October 1998, I and about ten other people waited six hours on the top floor of the Union Square Barnes and Noble in Manhattan for the arrival of Robert Jordan, the author of "The Wheel of Time" fantasy novel series. While waiting, some of us read his new book, *The Path of Daggers* (1998), while others read magazines or talked among each other about the works of Jordan. These fans were enthralled at the opportunity to meet the man behind the books, hear him read a passage, and then have him sign their brand-new copy of *The Path of Daggers*. Book signings are an important part of the science-fiction and fantasy world. As with all books, they allow the readers to share a connection with the person responsible for the work that captured their minds and hearts. To be sure, there is a sort of mythic quality around these events, an interaction between the audience and the writers, a connection to the unreachable, an insight into the life and mind of writers whom fans respect and admire. During the wait, the room began to fill up to the point that there were not enough chairs to accommodate the audience, and late arrivals were forced to stand in the back. An employee of Barnes and Noble would come up every once in a while to explain the rules of the book signing so that new arrivals would be given guidelines for expected proper behavior. At one point, as she stepped up to the podium, someone in the audience, perhaps annoyed at her repetitive announcements, shouted "Darkfriend!"—a reference to characters in Jordan's novels who work for Shai'Tan, the Dark One. This kind of behavior, along with all of the other events that occurred that evening—both before, during, and after the book signing—revealed a unique kind of performance.

The drama of the book signing, what Schechner would call the "written text," had its roots in *The Path of Daggers*, for Jordan would read from that book and audience members would have their copies of it signed. Also, the novel was the text around which the whole evening's performance was centered, which for many people was a culmination of a two-year wait for this book's publication. (Some people were even clutching two copies of the book.) This novel was also the basis for dramatic conversations among audience members as they waited. Fans passionately discussed various theories about the characters and plots, speculating about which plotlines would be developed and if particular secrets about characters would be revealed. One such topic was the question of whether or not Asmodean's killer was to be revealed. Asmodean was one of the forsaken, one of the Dark One's most powerful magicians. He was captured by Rand Al'Thor, who is the main character, and was shielded from his magical abilities by another of the forsaken so that he might teach Rand more about his own power. Near the end of the fifth book, he was murdered. His killer remains a mystery to this day, and we know only that the killer was someone he recognized. (Even this latest book did not reveal his killer, leaving further speculation until a later book.)

Finally, Robert Jordan walked into the room. The noise from the audience was deafening. He stepped up to the stage and was introduced by the "Darkfriend" employee as "The greatest American fantasy author." From somewhere within the sea of people a voice shouted "Amen!" which was followed by more shouting and thunderous applause. Then, after a brief speech, he began to read. The entire building, for the first time since I had been there six hours earlier, fell dead silent as Jordan read. For a book signing, an author must choose the passage that he or she feels best captures the spirit and intention of the book. There are often several passages that authors have singled out and must narrow down to one piece. In addition, authors must decide how to read a particular passage. Science fiction and fantasy tend to involve places, things, and languages that do not exist outside of the fantasy world comprising the novel, and the pronunciation of names of these things tends to differ from reader to reader. Therefore, one of the things that makes the reading special is that it allows the audience to hear these pronunciations from the man or woman who created these ideas. In that way, there is more of a connection to the work because readers can know that they are getting the correct pronunciation, making the imaginary world seem more familiar. During Jordan's performance, for example, he read the proper pronunciation of the Sea Folk, the Atha'an Miere. As he spoke this name, the audience was filled with a wave of different reactions. Some people sighed, while some nodded their heads in agreement. I said "yes" in a whisper and the person next to me nodded at me, recognizing that I would now be able to say the name correctly. We were all in awe of the man standing before us, the man whose novels we had devoted countless hours of our time to reading, and countless years to waiting for his next publication. The reading could not have been more than five minutes, but for me — and I am sure for everyone else around me, some of whom had been reading "The Wheel of Time" since they were no more then ten or eleven years old — it felt like hours.

Part of what makes the performance at a book signing so special is the level of awe and mystique around the author. It somehow brings a form to the abstract quality of the book itself, by revealing the person from whom the fantasy world was spawned. To the audience, the author is some-one who cannot be like everybody else. Seeing Robert Jordan read a selec-tion from his book is similar to the feeling one gets when seeing a famous celebrity they love, but have only seen in movies. Once he is seen in per-son, it becomes clear that Jordan is just another human being, me who hap-pens to have a job that allows his imagination to be seen in print by a vast majority of the general public.

After Jordan had finished reading his passage, the audience lined up to receive his autograph on their copies of *The Path of Daggers*. The looks on the faces of some of the people as they handed their books over to Mr. Jordan were unforgettable. Some people literally looked at him like slack-jawed gawkers, while others grinned uncontrollably. Some people tried to sneak in a question, even though it was forbidden by the Barnes and Noble employees. While I was up there, Jordan made some kind of remark about how, when he saw all of the people in the room, he thought maybe Stephen King was giving a book signing after him. Before I could get a hold of my tongue, I made some kind of remark about how I would not have come to meet Stephen King. I was stupefied by the fact that I was talking to a man who the day before had been nothing but a photo and a brief bio on the jacket cover of his books.

When I spoke to some of the members of the audience after the sign-ing, the adjectives they used to describe the performance ranged from "excellent" to "awesome" and "unbelievable." The answers I got from the store employees who witnessed the event ranged from "nice" all the way to "Well, we do so many of these that I don't really pay too much atten-tion anymore." The event ended, and the people filtered out of Barnes and Noble onto the streets of Manhattan to return to their ordinary lives.

PART III

Performing in Computer Games

The Performance
of War Games

BY BENJAMIN N. FOX

In 1811, Herr von Reiswitz, with the help of his son, a Prussian military officer, created the first war game as a way to train officers in the art of war. The game was called *Kriegspiel* and was loosely based on a popular game at the time called *War Chess*. It became a very successful training aid, and as other armies began to recognize the increasing skill of the Prussian military they soon created their own versions of *Kriegspiel*. The game took place on a sand table that was sculpted with hills and valleys to simulate realistic battlefield terrain, and the players strategically placed counters that represented different troop formations. A neutral overseer would determine the outcome of battles with the help of specific rules, and all random outcomes were determined by a roll of dice. Eventually the ideas of this military training method found their way into the lives of civilians as an entertaining recreational activity. H. G. Wells noticed the popularity of these war games and developed a game called *Little Wars* (1919). The biggest change that occurred was the replacement of the counters that were used in *Kriegspiel* by miniature figures. *Little Wars* was the first war game published for civilian consumers, and it defined the war games that would follow. In the search for combat reality, the armies in the games were outfitted with the military inventions of the period.

In order to develop more variety for enthusiasts, war game innovator Dave Wesely started to create ways for the games to be more than just battles of attrition. Wesely not only began to change the rules, but he also established scenarios for the conflicts. The different armies had individual goals that were more than merely an objective to "Kill them all!" Strategy became the key, and early games of this kind were filled with such complex tactics that they bordered on chaos. Wesely felt as though his attempt had been a failure, but those who had played felt quite the opposite. Dave Arneson picked up where Wesely left off and took war gaming to the world of the fantastic, creating medieval armies that were inspired by Tolkien's *The Lord of the Rings*. The miniature playing pieces evolved so that each model that once represented an entire unit now represented a single character. Gamers enthusiastically accepted this change. The armies were now filled with lots of different characters, including knights, dragons, mages, and kings. Through the addition of fantastic characters and massive armies, each game became a unique experience filled with action and suspense. Every move was carefully thought out because killing the enemy was not the only goal now; a story needed to be told. Gamers embraced the war games that had been created, and they wanted another way to express the lives of their characters. So, in response to this, Arneson teamed up with Gary Gygax — the co-creator of the game (with Jeff Perren) *Chainmail* (1971) — and together they created the world's first role-playing game, *Dungeons & Dragons*, which was published in 1974. Role-playing games affected the world of war gaming, and they both became dynamic entities that benefited from each other's existence.

As a result of this confluence of fantasy role-playing games and war gaming, over the past twenty years a new generation of war games has emerged. Such games as *Warhammer* take the players to totally new worlds through their all-encompassing rules systems and intricate miniatures. There are two variations of the game: *Warhammer 40000*, a futuristic war game populated by androids, genetically engineered humans, and parasitic aliens; and *Warhammer Fantasy Battle*, which is more akin to the original fantasy war games inspired by *The Lord of the Rings*. The designers of *Warhammer* created twenty races, each with its own characteristics, and rule books that describe the distinct personality of each army. The following quote is from *Realm of Chaos* (1990), a rule book for the armies of chaos. The particular army referred to is the army of Nurgle, which is an army of the demons of plague and pestilence:

> The Horde Travels in a great cavalcade of covered wagons, bringing with it all the pestilences and ills that befall the living. The wagons are in no better physical condition than the demons within. Their shrouds are tattered and rotten, their frames splintered and bent, and their metal-work pitted and rusted. Yet within the plodding caravan of Nurgle all is bustle and activity as the Great Unclean One prepares to launch a festival of decay and destruction upon a human village, a thriving town, or an opposing army. For Nurgle's visitation is like that of a traveling circus or great fair, except

that the entertainment it offers is disease, sickness, and death [Priestley & Ansell 1990:13].

Each army has a rule book written in a very specific tone that teaches not only the rules for the particular army but also how the army should behave. It is the vivid writing and the world that the writing creates that, perhaps, reveals war games as a type of performance.

According to Schechner, a performance consists of such parts as a drama, script, and theater (1988:72). In *Warhammer*, the drama includes the battle scenarios that can be found in the rule books. The rules also include instructions about how different characters interact, which comprises part of the script, which is "the basic code of events" (72). The battles in *Warhammer* are enacted in a turn-based system in which particular steps must be followed in a particular order:

1. MOVEMENT: Players decide how to move their troops. Each character (model) has specific movement abilities depending on many things, such as the amount of armor that it is wearing, if it is mounted on a horse or dragon, or even if the unit is going to engage another unit in combat. Moves are measured in inches, and the average unit moves four inches. If the average unit is wearing heavy armor, it may move only three inches. A horse can carry its rider eight inches, but a dragon can fly anywhere on the battlefield in a single movement phase. A player who wants to engage an enemy unit in combat must declare a charge, and the specified unit moves twice the normal rate toward the enemy.

2. SHOOTING: This is the phase when archers take aim and rain arrows down upon their foes. Dragons also use their breath weapon in this phase, be it frost or flame. The most frightening part of the shooting phase is when the war machines wreak havoc. This includes cannons, stonethrowers, and some even more diabolical inventions such as a giant slingshot that launches an explosive-carrying goblin into the air. Depending on the skill of a player, this can be the most devastating phase in a battle.

3. HAND-TO-HAND: Swords and axes are sharpened and warriors begin to hack at each other, hoping that shields and armor will protect them from death. Characters have statistics to determine how well they fight in combat and how many times they get to swing their sword.

4. MAGIC: From the shadows of the battlefield come the spell-casters. A roll of the dice determines how much magical energy is present for the mages to harness. Using this energy, they unleash the powers that they have studied for ages. There are many different paths of magic: light, dark, and chaos are just a few. Mages also have the ability to counter other magic.

5. RALLY: The final phase of a single turn. This is when the gamemaster — the referee of the game — tallies up how much damage was done in the turn. If a unit lost too many troops, then the player needs to roll dice to determine if the unit flees in panic. It is also a time when the player can attempt to calm the fleeing troops by a die roll. These five steps comprise the script that is repeated until the battle is over. Victory terms are set at the beginning of the battle by the gamemaster.

The theater of war for this kind of event comprises the actions taken by the players on the battlefield. For example, an army of humans may invade an Elven temple that houses an ancient artifact of great power. Turn by turn, the event is played out until there is a victor. In *Warhammer* the theater is created through lush illustrative language, intricate models, and the sheer chaos that ensues when a battle really gets going. The idea of war itself brings with it a certain magnitude, but in the particular instance of a war game the amount of chaos that is created when armies collide on the battlefield is quite sufficient to create the feeling of a massive conflict. Before the creation of the individual soldier representations, the conflict seemed definitely smaller. Having fifteen or so tokens to represent an army seems much less powerful than having six units of fifteen heavily armored warriors and mounted knights, backed up by two cannons and their crew with a mystical sorcerer in the rear, overseeing the foray. These metal-cast figures are set on a table that is covered with trees and streams. The more the players do to create a realistic-looking army and battlefield, the more it will directly affect their perception of the magnitude of the battle.

Today's figures in the different armies and characters seem to be full of life and individual personality, and are unlike the thimble in *Monopoly*, for example, which generically represents any player. The descriptive passages, such as the quote from the *Realm of Chaos* cited earlier, define the character of each different army and provide each army with a distinct personality, offering the players a particularized role to play that is similar to a role-playing game. When these characters meet on the battlefield, a certain energy is created similar to the energy created when the protagonist and antagonist first meet in a stage play. When mystic High Elves encounter a noble Brentonian army, a certain kind of battle ensues that is much different from when ravenous orcs meet up with a shambling undead hoard. Embodying the roles of the their respective armies, players may even taunt one another as they move their pieces, performing the verbal tropes of elves, orcs, and other fantastic beings. This is an example of just how dynamic the world of a war game can be. It is the responsibility of the gamers (or role-players), however, to raise the game from the mundane to the point of performance.

Playing Video Games as a Performance

BY CHRISTOPHER SHADE

Since the beginning of time, humans have sought to assume other characters. The Greeks fancied themselves playing gods in their arenas, and in Shakespeare's time men desired the role of king. Even today there is a strong desire to become something else, and the imagination is the only limit. With the advent of movies in the early twentieth century, other worlds could be realistically depicted as if they were true places, but the difficulty with movies (as well as with stage plays) is that there was no way for the spectator to control the action. However, in a video game, not only is the alternate universe depicted realistically like in a movie, it is also in the hands of the video game player. Within this medium, players can actually perform characters, since they are given a role or mission and must strive to complete it.

There are two different kinds of video games: those that try to depict reality as closely as possible, and those that create a totally different world with the player's character in the center of the action. The first of these two types consists mainly of sports and racing games, which get more realistic every year, while the latter type continues to push the limits of imagination. These non-realistic games feature slimy aliens, ghoulish ghosts, people with special powers, and magical weapons, consisting of science-fiction and fantasy tropes found previously in novels, film, and television. One can do everything from flying a spaceship to killing Martians to saving the universe. As appealing as all of this may sound, these types do not generally outsell reality-based games. There is one exception to that rule, however. The game *Colony Wars* has had outstanding and consistent sales ever since it came out in 1997. The only thing that might surpass it is its own sequel, which was released in late 1998. In the video game business, for a game to sell consistently after its first few months is a rare and definite sign of success.

But why is this game so popular? It does not have any movie tie-ins, nor does it feature anything or anyone famous or well known. The answer to that question lies in the presentation of the game and its role in the general scheme of video games as an entertainment genre. If one looks at video games as a performance, then they can be analyzed using Schechner's theories of how a performance works. As well, one can tie in theories of the psychological aspects of why video games affect people with such compulsion. Still the question remains of why this particular game has such a draw in the marketplace. There are certainly more appealing games, like those based on *Star Wars* and *Star Trek*. Upon further review of what makes a performance work, one can discover that *Colony Wars* relates to the player by using familiar story lines and characters from popular science-fiction films and television shows. It couples this with game play that is exciting because it puts the players in the middle of a story and gives them a role beyond that of audience members. They are, in fact, the central figure in the plot and must push the story along without dying, and complete the mission.

Video games started back in the late 1970s with the introduction of a game called *Pong*, which is an electronic version of table tennis. Upon its introduction at a bar in the San Francisco Bay Area, it was an immediate success ... until it broke. When the designer came to fix it, he found that the mechanisms of the game were jammed because the quarter tray was overflowing with quarters. Since then the popularity of video games increased rapidly. Graphics got better, and arcades were formed where kids and adults could spend their hard-earned money on such electronic games as *Pac-Man* and *Asteroids*. It was not until the popularity of the Atari Video Computer System, which plugged into a television set, that games had a significant effect on the home market, selling more than ten million units in the early 1980s. Atari was the first system that allowed people to switch cartridges, making the possibility for available games endless. The Atari VCS (later called the Atari 2600) was just the beginning of home systems. Pretty soon there was such an influx of games and hardware that the entire industry "crashed" in 1984, leaving arcades as the only popular venue for games.

In 1986, Nintendo entered the market with the Nintendo Entertainment System and the business boomed once again. Nintendo learned from the mistakes of previous companies and regulated the number of games that were available for release. Seeing the success of Nintendo, a software company named Sega came out with their own system, called the Sega Master System. Since then, each company has made numerous advancements in its hardware and released systems with better graphics and more realism. The invention of the compact disk (CD) was vital to the growth of the systems and the industry in general because of the CD's storage capacity. Sega was the first to use this technology, first in its Sega CD system and then later in its Sega Saturn. Nintendo has yet to utilize this technology, even though it has made great advancements with cartridges. Other companies have also come and gone in this marketplace. Neo-Geo, NEC, and Panasonic have all tried to jump on the video game bandwagon, but they have not succeeded for a variety of reasons, such as poor marketing and high cost. One company that has exceeded all predictions to become the biggest player in the video game market is Sony. With its Playstation, Sony has reigned with a library of more than four hundred titles released in America, some of which are the most successful games of all time.

To understand how a game can be successful in terms of popularity and sales, one must first examine the subject matter of the game and study how it is presented. Once the game *Colony Wars* is placed in a Playstation, for example, a screen appears that shows the title and credits the creators of the game alongside a picture of a scene from the game. Then, there is an animation sequence that is meant to give an introduction and background to the story. The animation graphics are different from the actual game graphics and allow for more smoothness in textures and more vivid colors. Then a deep voice (which sounds remarkably like James Earl Jones, the voice of Darth Vader from *Star Wars*) comes on and begins to give a brief history, which serves as the prologue to the game. The story is a familiar one depicting the Earth Empire as a hostile alliance with absolute power over its subjects. The alliance travels from planet to planet with its destructive navy, colonizing and taking them over with no regard to life or well-being. In response, a rebel alliance has formed called the League of Free Worlds; their mission is to stop the Earth Empire from taking over any more lands. At the start of the game the League has just defeated the Empire in a critical battle at Bennay and is now a formidable foe of the evil Empire.

After the introductory animation, the screen changes to one that features four different words with one of them highlighted. By moving the controller, the player can choose which option to use next. The player may then "Adjust Options," "Reset the Game," "Show a Demo," or "Log On." When the player logs on, a new screen appears—similar to the previous one—allowing the player to choose from a new menu. This menu features databases of the player and the spacecraft in the game, as well as the option to begin a mission. When a player is ready to begin the game, the selection of "Begin Campaign" is made and that player will be given a briefing about the mission and its directives. The missions start out with one simple task, but they get more and more complex as the game progresses. All missions take place in the cockpit of various starcraft and are based on fighting other ships. One may also choose training missions to hone flight and combat skills.

At any point throughout the game, the *League Manual* may be consulted. This booklet comes in the package with the game. It details what all of the options mean and provides instructions for how to play the game and use the controls. The controller has a stick, two directional buttons, four weapons buttons, and two thrust buttons. It is this controller that is the player's link to the game. Without it, the player would have no control over the game except for turning it on and off.

In *Performance Theory* (1988), Schechner applies specific definitions to drama, script, theater, and performance. He writes that drama is the "domain of the author, the composer, scenarist, shaman" (71). For *Colony Wars*, the "author" would be the game creators, writers, and animators. Instead of just writing words, composing music, and visualizing pictures (all of which are included), the creators also write code. Code is the language the computer reads and translates into movement, voice, and animations. An example of this is the story line animations. At certain points in the game, the plot unravels through animations. Each animation is a computer-generated mini-movie, which is a set translation of code that the player has no control over. Each one is always the same, since it is fixed code "burned" onto the CD.

The script of the game, which includes all of the drama, also branches out to include the strategy surrounding the game and the reviews and opinions made about the game. The script is the "how to" of performance — "the basic code of events" or "patterns of doing" (Schechner 1988:70). This includes all of the "potential manifestations" of the ships and their movement. It also includes all of the controls outlined in the *League Manual*. All of these potential actions are transmitted to each player in a different way and are subject to interpretation. The best example of a piece of the script of a game is the strategy guide. Most games, after they are released, have a strategy guide attributed to them. This is a separate book that give detailed maps, secrets, and the most effective ways of finishing the game. It is written by someone or a group of people who have played through the game and have been helped by the creators. There are also websites and magazines that give helpful hints and comments about the game, adding to the script of the performance. All of these guides are ways in which the actions of the game, effectively the script, may be used to provide desired results.

Another element that Schechner describes is theater, which includes the performers and the concrete actions they perform to represent the drama by means of a script. In *Colony Wars*, the performers are animated characters as well as the player, and the theater is the realm in which they perform. This includes the starcraft, the actual battles, and the results of the outcome of each mission. It is also, as Schechner describes, "the event enacted by a specific group of performers; what the performers actually do during production. The theater is concrete and immediate. Usually, the theater is the manifestation of the drama and/or script" (1988:72). After reading the *League Manual*, watching the introduction videos, and getting a mission briefing, a player is ready to take part in the theater of *Colony Wars*. This happens when the player begins a battle and takes control of the ship. Using the controller and the moves that it allows, a player enacts a scene. One of the best scenes is in Galloniah, where there is a huge space station resembling the Death Star from *Star Wars*. The player must shoot down all of the ships launched from the station, then disable it, making it vulnerable for takeover. As the player shoots down the other ships, the scene unravels and is either advantageous for the League or a mission failure, depending on the enactment of the script as performed by the player.

The last element that Schechner outlines in his essay is the all-encompassing performance, "the whole constellation of events" (1988:72). This is everything that concerns the playing of *Colony Wars*, from turning on the Playstation to finally quitting and leaving the game. The most important element of the performance is the player, who acts as an audience member as well as a participant. Though players control the action onscreen, they are sometimes not a part of the performance. It is tricky to differentiate between the two, since the character that the player controls is a part of the performance event. This separation can be seen in the event of "trash-talking," when the player (or any audience member watching) yells at the screen. This is definitely an important part of the performance and adds great excitement to it. For example, the audience may respond with anger: "Damn you!" or praise: "Yes! Woo-hoo!" or instruction: "C'mon, shoot them!" All of these outbursts are part of the performance, yet they do not affect the game play at all. The ships will not fly faster if the player tells them to do so. The controller remains the player's only connection to the action onscreen.

One aspect of the game that separates it from other performances is the length of time it can be performed. Very few people can sit down in front of the television and play this game from beginning to end without stopping. For one, it is difficult and takes some practice over time to master the controller movements. Also, it is a long game with many missions. Therefore, most players will save the game on a memory card and come back to it at a later date. This essentially freezes the performance at some specific point to be resumed later. Similar to this aspect is the replay option. Since a game can be saved, the designers of the game intentionally make it difficult for someone to succeed on the first attempt. Thus, there are many times when a person will die in combat and have to begin again at the last "save" point. This separates the play of Colony Wars from any other kind of more traditional drama or theater. At no point does conventional theater force the performers to repeat the action. The closest thing that can be ascribed to this process of redoing is the rehearsal process in which a scene is gone over time and time again until it is right for performance. However, since the game mixes the role of spectator with that of performer, the rehearsals can be considered part of the performance.

Now that Colony Wars can be viewed from the perspective of a performance, possessing all of the qualities a performance should have, it becomes possible to analyze its success as such. Although the video game genre in general is naturally popular, it may be crucial to ask why Colony Wars is successful in its field. Critical to an understanding of this, of course, is that video games allow the player to be a performer. The player can enter and become a part of another world, a world in which there is an immediate crisis that must be remedied. Either someone has been kidnapped, or a race is begun, or in the case of Colony Wars, a war is currently being fought. Whatever the situation, the game drops the player smack dab into the middle of it. This allows for immediate urgency on the part of the player. Even if the remedy is not resolved during many hours or even days of game play, the urgency is always there. It is a problem that must be solved. The reasons Colony Wars works on this level are twofold. On the one hand, the cause is noble and epic. The entire free universe is in the hands of a few pilots, and they must save it. On the other hand, the cause is personal to human morality. What the Empire is doing is essentially wrong, and it must be stopped at all costs.

The reason why Colony Wars is so popular among video game players nationwide is the same reason that great drama is popular. It provides a familiar story that relates to human existence. The elements of the story are essentially human elements and tell a familiar story to which players can relate. This story is one of the underdog, who is oppressed, comes back, and defeats a huge powerful empire. Unlike traditional drama, a video game story makes a player not only relate to the story, but also became a part of it, controlling the action. That would be like telling Hamlet what to do because you play Hamlet.

Finally, it is necessary to discuss *Colony Wars* with regard to the influences that it obviously has taken from its predecessors. It is the familiarity with these influences that further adds to its success. When players take control of the ship in *Colony Wars*, they are fighting for the very same principles that led Luke Skywalker and the rebellion in *Star Wars*. Even the names are similar, and in the introductory narrative it is no coincidence that the voice sounds like that of Darth Vader. Another aspect similar to the popular forerunners is the design of the ships. Many of them look very similar to the ships found in *Star Wars* and *Star Trek*. All of these similarities are no coincidence. By making images that are familiar to the players, the creators of *Colony Wars* hoped to engulf the players into the game play quicker and easier. By providing a story line that is familiar and images that reinforce the way space travel and combat are perceived, *Colony Wars* easily captivates its audience, since they do not have to imagine new types of images or reasons to fight.

By combining the aspects of performance that make drama so captivating and interesting to watch and be a part of, *Colony Wars* stands out among video games as one that is extremely successful. It is arranged in such a way as to allow players to have complete control over the environment and to be submerged in a world that is full of problems that only they can solve. The game also works since its problems are not isolated to the confines of the fantasy world in which they take place, but are essentially the problems that plague humankind, namely, oppression and discrimination. This in turn makes the player strive to put a fictional end to these problems by taking the driver's seat and facing them head-on — since many are unable to do so in real life. In the end, if all goes well, the League triumphs and there is peace. And the pleasure of the game comes not only from the attainment of victory; if one fails, there is always the reset button.

The Re-performance
of Star Wars
in Computer Games

BY KELLEE SANTIAGO

> *Throughout the inhabited world, in all times and under every cir-*
> *cumstance, the myths of man have flourished; and they have been*
> *the living inspiration of whatever else may have appeared out of*
> *the activities of the human body and mind.*
> —Joseph Campbell, *The Hero with a Thousand Faces* (1968)

Whenever *Star Wars* merchandise is released, a mass of humanity flocks to buy whatever is being sold. Selling *Star Wars* merchandise is easy money. However, while it might be true that the *Star Wars* label does grab many people's attention, there is something more that drives them to go out and purchase it. The fans of *Star Wars* have gone beyond loving the plot of the films on a film-appreciation level; they wish to be immersed within the *Star Wars* universe. To protect the films' content from overexposure, the *Star Wars* computer games are never allowed to touch the story and main characters of the films, so game designers have ventured far from it by expanding the universe. The computer games cannot and do not coincide with the films. So, fans do not purchase them to enter the story of the films, but to become a part of the universe of *Star Wars*. Graeme Turner, in *Film as Social Practice* (1988), explains how films should allow for a certain universality so that they may be reproduced and re-performed in society: "Popular films have a life beyond their theater runs or their reruns on television ... in [their] narratives and meaning we can locate evidence of the ways in which our culture makes sense of itself" (xv).

The *Star Wars* universe has been taken from the films and then re-created, expanded, and combined with the performance possibilities of computer technology so that fans are able to perform within the *Star Wars* universe. Through computer games, *Star Wars* fans manipulate "strips of behavior" (as Schechner has described) that allow them to perform in their own way within that universe. The examples are plentiful, but three prime examples of how a computer game can cause an audience member to enter the universe of *Star Wars* and take part in it are *X-Wing v. Tie-Fighter* (1997), *Dark Forces* (1994), and *Star Warped* (1997).

Star Wars is so easily re-performed because George Lucas used ancient myths as his blueprints, giving the films a certain universality. Campbell explains in *The Power of Myth* that "the main motif of the myths are the same, and they have always been the same" (1991:27). There are very basic themes of good and evil throughout the films, which can be easily repro-duced by game designers. The same myths that Lucas used to create the films can also be used by the designers to not only re-create the perfor-mance of the films, but to expand upon them. As long as the designers con-tinue playing under Lucas's rules, any situation is possible in the *Star Wars* universe. Because Lucas created the *Star Wars* universe as, literally, a uni-verse, it can be easily re-performed. Mary Henderson explains: "The 'alter-nate reality' that helps to place the *Star Wars* saga in the realm of myth is certainly part of its magic. But Lucas didn't just settle for creating a new universe, whose every culture comes complete with its own laws, land-scapes, and history; he also set his adventure in an alternate time" (1997:10). By setting the films "a long time ago, in a galaxy far, far away," Lucas allowed for just about anything to happen in the films. In creating them, he laid down a ground plan of rules for that universe. Thus, game design-ers took these rules and played around with them as much as they wanted because the setting was so removed from our reality, creating limitless options.

By taking certain scenic concepts or character ideas, a game designer can re-create the *Star Wars* universe in a completely different medium, one in which the audience is allowed to interact with the universe. For example, in *X-Wing v. Tie-Fighter*, named after the fighter spacecraft in *Star Wars*, the plot of the game takes place immediately before the *Star Wars* trilogy begins. You can be either a member of the Empire and fight for it, or a member of the Rebel Alliance. The first interface that brings the audi-ence into the world of *Star Wars* is the initial "log in" page. The player has to create a pilot name or choose one that he or she has already begun. On the right-hand side of the screen, there is a "Pilot Roster" list consisting of any previously saved pilot names.

The entire game screen of *X-Wing v. Tie-Fighter* consists of dark colors such as black, dark silver, and dark blue, with the bright color of the text typing in the center of the screen. These colors can be associated with either X-Wings or Tie-Fighters, because in the films the cockpits of both crafts were decorated with dark colors. However, since the audience never got a very clear view of the cockpits of either craft, the programmer can invent any system to fit the game on a functional level and then decorate it to create a performance for the player. Players are allowed to choose which side they want to fight for and what craft they want to fly. Because players have these options, they feel like important members of that universe. By deciding sides, players can choose who will win the entire war. In this way, they can participate in the *Star Wars* films by assisting the Rebel Alliance, or they can change the plot by helping the Empire to win. These endings assume that players will be good enough to win each battle. They could also change the plot by fighting for the Alliance and then losing, allowing the Empire to win. In another, more far-reaching option, players can participate in a game through the internet. Players from all over the world choose sides and fight in intergalactic battles. This option heightens the performance because players get to interact with other players live. It is similar to the difference between an actor performing a monologue to an imaginary person and an actor performing the same monologue to another actor. The performer gets to interact with a live opponent, and of course real people will use much different tactics than the computer.

The game *Dark Forces* also has a plot that takes place immediately before the films begin. The player performs as a Rebel Alliance member who has been a rebel of his own — similar to Han Solo's role in the films — in a first person–style computer game, where what one sees on the screen is from the perspective of the player. The game begins with a signature *Star Wars* trope: "A Long Time Ago, in a Galaxy Far, Far, Away..." Then the *Star Wars* logo appears on the computer screen and the opening music begins, just as in the introduction to all the *Star Wars* films. The events that "occurred" before the game are then revealed just as the preceding plots of the films are, in the scrolling yellow text with a starry background. Through this trope, the players are immediately brought into the *Star Wars* universe. However, they have not interacted in it, but merely entered into it, not yet taking any action in performing within it. As this scrolling script goes by, the player learns that the Rebel Alliance has just gained knowledge of the Death Star, but they have been unable to get any information on it though their usual contacts. The Alliance has decided to hire Kyle Katarn, who has worked independently with the Imperials. As the script disappears, just like the beginning of *Star Wars*, the music softens and the screen scrolls down the starry sky to reveal the Death Star hovering over a large blue planet. As in the film, a blue-gray starship flies over the "camera" and off into the distance.

The next scene is a series of quick shots of a man's waist as he loads up his gun and puts ammunition in his belt. These shots most successfully integrate the player into the game by recalling action movies with similar shots. It is obvious at this point that this is the character of the player, and that he is a "good guy," despite his possibly troubled background. Also, in integrating the two genres of the first-person shooter games (such as *Doom*) and *Star Wars*, there has to be some successful connection. Though *Star Wars* is action-packed, there is not nearly the amount of mass slaughter that takes place in a *Doom* game. *Doom* lacks any deep plot that *Star Wars* requires. In this brief series of shots, the world of *Star Wars* is presented through the quick, action-style nature of the shots and the style of clothing the character is wearing, and then elements of *Doom* are added upon it when the character is given a tough attitude through the focus on the gun and ammunition. It is apparent that there is to be some "kick-ass" killing in this game.

The screen then switches into a more formal setting for the mission briefing. There is a black background, and on the left side of the screen there is the image of Senator Mon Mothma, the female leader of the Rebel Alliance from *Return of the Jedi*. On the right top corner of the screen in red type there is a header: "Prologue Mission I/The Death Star Plans/Operation Skyhook: Phase 2." Then directly below the header, there is green type explaining, "Confidential Message from Senator Mon Mothma." It goes on to describe the player's mission: to find the plans for the Death Star for Princess Leia. There is a small image that appears to be a map of the area the player will be searching, but it is not very detailed and appears to exist only for the purpose of enhancing the feeling that this is an official mission briefing. This official facade is continued as the player scrolls down the screen through the mission briefing, and at the end of it in blue font the screen reads, "Mission Objectives." This screen finally pulls the player directly into the *Star Wars* universe. Also, not only does it pull the participant in, but it orders the player to take a place in the universe to help it survive. The player is given a character and an action to perform (just as in any play or film).

There is another style of performance, however, that brings the audience into the *Star Wars* universe. *Star Warped* presents a premise of two *Star Wars* fans, Brian and Aaron, who have created a computer game in which one can explore their room full of *Star Wars* paraphernalia, play games they have created, and watch secret video tapes they got from the

"Ranch Cam," that is, from video cameras overlooking Skywalker Ranch, where George Lucas and his team work on his films. The introduction to the universe is like that of *Dark Forces*, but with a twist. Instead of the classic line, "A long time ago, in a galaxy far, far, away," this game begins with a different line, "Two-and-a-half weeks ago in a bedroom in Modesto…" (Lucas's hometown). This line is represented exactly like the classic line from the films—black background and yellow font — so the audience sees it and immediately associates this "strip of behavior" with the *Star Wars* films. However, since the words are changed, it clues the player in to the entire style of the game. This computer game still allows the player to re-perform in the *Star Wars* universe, but it also breaks some of the rules of the universe for comedic value and pure entertainment. There are no stakes involved as high as saving the Rebel Alliance, but participants can play a game of "Whack an Ewok." The re-performance also allows players to break rules of the universe, and so gives them a sense of having power and control over it, instead of being subject to it as in the games previously mentioned.

These computer games all take "certain strips of behavior," as explained by Schechner, from the universe of the *Star Wars* films and then add to them to create an interactive environment, allowing the audience of the game to perform within that universe. *X-Wing v. Tie-Fighter* limits the performance to space battles, but it does allow the player to choose a side. *Dark Forces* assigns the player a specific character and also behavior, but it also lets the player interact with more characters from the movies, such as Senator Mon Mothma. Finally, *Star Warped* does not involve itself in the "real" universe of the films, but takes common ideas and conceptions and allows the player to play around as a fan and break the rules for a little while. The three games allow for interaction in different ways, serving the needs of different types of audiences. However, every audience member is searching for the same basic thing: to perform and interact within the *Star Wars* universe. People do not play these games simply for their love of the films or any collector value, but for the chance to be a part of a universe that they have enjoyed watching from a distance for so long.

Virtual Simulated Environments: Performing in "*The Ages of* Myst *and* Riven"

BY TOM MIKOTOWICZ

It was in 1970 that Alvin Toffler, in his prescient book *Future Shock*, predicted the basic human desire to experience simulated environments "that offer the customer a taste of adventure, danger, sexual titillation, or other pleasure without risk to his real life or reputation" (228). This future vision of popular culture theorized that "customers entering these pleasure domes will leave their everyday clothes (and cares) behind, don costumes, and run through a planned sequence of activities intended to provide them with a first-hand taste of what the original — i.e. ... unsimulated environment — must have felt like. They will be invited, in effect, to live in the past or perhaps even in the future" (228). Although one can argue that the idea of simulated environments has been with us since the first pagan festivals — carnivals, theme parks, and the like — the world is not quite at the point of total immersion and illusion that Toffler envisioned. However, through the computer interface it is becoming possible to experience a virtual idea of that sense of immersion, while temporarily suspending ordinary life and becoming immersed in some fantasy land as a character created by a team of programmers. The popularity of computerized simulated environments is without question, and is especially apparent in the CD-ROM–based games *Myst* and *Riven*, by Cyan Software, which have sold in the millions to fans across the globe.

Before we discuss the games, some focus must be put on the confusion that surrounds the use of such terms as *simulated* and *virtual. Simulated* suggests something artificial or unreal. However, a simulated environment may not appear to be what it actually is, but it certainly is a real environment—one into which an individual can enter and with which one can interact. Such past television shows and films as *Fantasy Island* and *Westworld*, showing human beings living in the simulated circumstances of Paradise and the Wild West, are good examples of this. The word *virtual*, on the other hand, has suggested something that is not in three dimensions in the physical world. Nonetheless, a virtual environment is, in fact, actual in terms of its use. For example, a computer can become a virtual bank when someone goes online and transfers funds, or someone can have a virtual conference on the internet without actually being in the same room with the other participants. Thus, a chat room, with our current technology, is a virtual room, and not necessarily an actual one. It is made of electronic bits and bytes and disappears after logging off or shutting down the computer system. One does not enter into the virtual environment physically, and it does not necessarily (or always) pretend to be some other environment, aesthetically. A virtual simulated environment, however, does pretend to be some other environment.

Moreover, the difference between a simulated room and a virtual chat room can be seen in the simulated environment of a cooking show that takes place in a supposed kitchen that is constructed in a television studio. The actual refrigerator, sink, and stove may, in fact, work, and the counter and cupboards make it look like a kitchen, but it does not have its own ceiling and it is taken down after the show and packed away. Even though one can freeze food in the refrigerator and actually cook things on the stove, these are only there to simulate a kitchen. However, this "kitchen" exists in the real world and is subject to the physical laws of science, while in virtual environments, objects are not actually there and can only simulate being subject to the actual physical laws, or even not subject to them. In a virtual environment things work, but they only work in the context of the virtual world, not the real one. Thus, one can burn oneself on the stove in the simulated kitchen, but one cannot die by crashing one's airship in the virtual simulated environment of the computer game *Wing Commander*.

That is what makes virtual environments so much fun and less dangerous than simulated ones with our current technology. Of course, Toffler's vision of the future emphasizes that a customer would experience the simulated environment without risk of injury, death, or loss of reputation. With virtual environments that future is already here, albeit perhaps not as much fun as Toffler's truly simulated environments will be in the future.

Virtual environments, however, can simulate to a high degree through their interface, which is the computer. Through elaborate graphics, sounds, and animation, various environments can be constructed for the viewers/players that immerse them into another world, one in which the physical laws of science do not limit human activity. Such games as *Wing Commander*, *Half-Life*, and *Silent Hill* seek to create other environments that range from the science-fictionalized to the horrific. Currently, there are no simulated environments to the degree that Toffler describes, but there are entertainment environments that contain rides or attractions, such as Disney World's "Alien" or Universal Studio Theme Park's "Jurassic Park," that put the spectator into a simulated environment. These, however, may someday be considered primitive attempts at truly simulated environments because the immersion of the spectator is limited to being shuttled through a thrilling ride rather than experiencing an intellectual or emotional involvement through complex characters or situations. This would be like comparing late-nineteenth-century stereopticons with the present film industry. Until Disney or some other mega-entertainment corporation creates a "Fantasy Island" or a *Star Trek: The Next Generation* holodeck, where participants can adopt a character, set out to accomplish an objective, and interact with purpose with the environment, Toffler's future vision will not be fully realized. In the meantime, there is the next best thing, computerized games — the virtual environments created by the computer interface. For the purposes of this article then, both *Myst* and *Riven* are virtual environments that simulate because you cannot really enter into them physically, and their locales exist only in cyberspace. Therefore, they are not truly simulated environments as will exist in the future.

The first game of the two created by the team of Rand and Robyn Miller was *Myst*, which was released by Broderbund Software in 1993, sold millions of copies, and won countless awards from various computer and publishing associations, as well as garnered kudos from mainstream media. Although throughout the 1980s there had been adventure games in primitive computer form as well as in other media, *Myst* was unique because the player could advance through a virtual environment that seemed mysterious, but one without overtly challenging puzzles, violent combat, or dangerous situations. In *Myst* the emphasis was on discovery through intelligently exploring the unusual surrealistic island upon which the player is virtually dropped at the start of the game. Thus, in a more realistic fashion, the puzzles within the game had to be discovered as well as solved.

For their next project, the Miller brothers procured another partner, Richard Vander Wende, together with a significantly increased staff of artists and computer personnel to create an even larger virtual environment with *Riven*. This game came out in 1997 and has equaled, if not surpassed, the fame of *Myst*, both in fans' enthusiasm and in economic success. *Riven*'s scenario continues the plot and characters from the first game but takes the viewer into another world of five islands, each of which must be explored to find the ultimate solution. Although both games demanded much of computer technology to graphically illustrate the virtual environments, *Riven* was a definite advancement over *Myst* in the development of computer techniques, software, and equipment for rendering the other worlds, and it took a few years longer and more resources to develop. In fact, *Riven*'s graphic renderings for the virtual environment totaled more than 4,000 drawings as opposed to *Myst*'s 2,500 drawings.

The fictive story line that draws a player into both games surrounds the activities of a family, in which there is betrayal, imprisonment, and domination. Despite the lack of violence, it is almost worthy of being compared to a Greek or Shakespearean tragedy, and it has characters who appear as live performers in some of the filmed action sequences in the game. They are the evil Gehn, his son Atrus, Atrus's wife, Catherine, and their two sons, Sirrus and Achenaar. The ultimate objective surrounds the imprisonment of Gehn, avoidance of the scheming sons, and the rescue of Atrus and Catherine by the player.

Undoubtedly, in a traditional sense, the player's involvement in *Myst* and *Riven* can be considered a theatrical performance. Without having to adopt a fictive character role, though, the player sets out to achieve an objective much like Oedipus, who must find out what is causing the plague in Thebes, or Hamlet, who must find out if his uncle really did kill his father, seduce his mother, and usurp the throne. In *An Actor Prepares*, the early-twentieth-century acting theorist Konstantin Stanislavski noted that the basic action of a theatrical character was the "creative objective" (1936:110). Throughout the games of *Myst* and *Riven*, the player is given an objective that carries him or her through all of the various locales in the virtual environments. As Richard Kadrey makes clear in his *From* Myst *to* Riven: *The Creations & Inspirations*, "what really sucks the player in is that there is a deeply felt purpose to playing the game" (1997:81). This purpose is introduced through various books in *Myst*, as well as directly by Atrus at the beginning of *Riven*, who tells the player what has happened and what needs to be done. Most importantly, this purpose also makes significant the exploration of even the tiniest details of the journey and carries the player through the long and arduous process of covering the many locales in the games. In fact, all of the "scenography" and "props" were designed and rendered to reveal character and information that would lead the player to achieving the objectives of the games. This is not dis-similar to a theatrical designer, operating under twentieth-century organic unity, bringing the moods, character, and feeling of the play out in the design of the costumes, settings, sound, and lighting. Thus, the player starts with an objective and is "fed" information visually and aurally throughout his or her progress of the game to achieve the goal.

The use of theatrical time and space in each game is essentially non-traditional, in that it is nonlinear, interdimensional, and interactive. The virtual environment of each game is largely made up of paths that move through the mountains, jungles, buildings, lakes, oceans, machinery, bridges, and vehicles of the islands, as well as from dimension to dimension throughout the different ages and worlds of the games. By viewing the computer monitor and clicking with the mouse, the player moves through the environments, turning and opening dials, levers, books, and doors along the way in an effort to learn how to advance to a new level in the game. The player can move through the game in a nonlinear fashion, advancing forward yet with the ability to move backward and retrace his or her steps. The time is actual, but sometimes it includes the symbolic or fictive time of the characters and plot. For the player's reality, performance time can be segmented or serialized because the games are not played in one sitting. In fact, they have a level of difficulty such that some players can take years to complete the games. Thus, the progression toward the character's objective is usually intermittent — when it is convenient to play the game, rather than continuous.

In the progressive sense, as outlined by theorist Richard Schechner in his essay "Drama, Script, Theatre, and Performance," the CD-ROM games of *Myst* and *Riven* can be analyzed as performance (1988:72). Certainly there is a drama, consisting of what the Miller brothers created in terms of the conflict among the fictional family members, and which is the map or plan. In fact, in the games it is literally the map and plan of the islands and other worlds that guides the performance. The script is the CD-ROM with the attendant characters, which teaches the performer/spectator all there is to know regarding the performance. The computer teaches the player, who, already knowledgeable of a Windows interface, quickly learns how to move through the drama — and that is what become the "patterns of doing" and the embodiment of action as Schechner says occurs in conventional drama. The theatre is the actual playing of the game, which can take on different qualities depending upon the various players and can elicit many different responses. Finally, the performance is the phenomenon of *Myst* and *Riven*, including the actual playing of the games, websites, discussion groups, and books.

In terms of this latter element, a broader cultural perspective on the exceptional success of these games reveals that many of the beliefs of our society seem to be embodied in them. As noted cultural anthropologist Victor Turner has suggested, all of the values and goals of a culture are inherent in its performances (Schechner and Appel 1990:1). So, too, in *Myst* and *Riven*, various themes and values are revealed, such as the fact that good can triumph over evil, domination of other cultures is inherently bad, and technology can be used either for good or evil depending upon who is in charge. What decent human being would not want to rescue Catherine and imprison the villainous Gehn? Players buy into the fact that they represent good over evil, and that they can overcome even the most difficult of challenges to do so. This, of course, is notwithstanding the fact that the *Official* Myst *[and* Riven*] Hints and Solutions* books have sold an enormous amount of copies at such mall stores as Border's Books, Staples, B. Dalton, and Electronic Boutique. Thus, for the "heroically or intellectually challenged players" there is assistance with the more difficult puzzles. Nevertheless, the deeper codes of our culture are embedded in the games and attract the player into the immersion.

William Shatner, of Captain Kirk fame, in various interviews mentioned that he has been asked why *Star Trek* was so successful. His answer was that he believed in what Joseph Campbell has pointed out in his writings, that when a culture no longer believes in the great myths of its traditions, it seeks new myths in which to believe. The games, much like *Star Trek* and Tolkien's *The Lord of the Rings* trilogy, provide a cultural mythical structure in which to immerse oneself, worlds with distinctly positive values and a hero's journey worth taking. The player experiences the whole culture of the D'ni (pronounced "dunny") with their language, numbering system, and belief system, all of which are not much different in many ways from that of any decent culture. Additionally, the desire of the fans to transcend their everyday existence and enter into *Myst*'s and *Riven*'s virtual environments fulfills the need to perform, which many from Aristotle to Andy Warhol have claimed is intrinsic to human behavior (Dukore 1974:xx). Even Toffler realized that these simulated environments would be popular for people because they could perform and interact directly rather than vicariously through a fictive character as in a book or film (1970:229).

The future of truly simulated environments depends on this next wave of virtual ones because it would take the coming together of new technologies in film, computers, and other media to create the ultimate in simulation. *Myst* and *Riven* are important stages in this evolution because they have gone beyond the fantasy of Tolkien's book about Middle-earth and have put the spectator into a firsthand experience (and intellectual combat) with the D'ni and Gehn himself. The twentieth-century passivity of the spectator has given way to a postmodern, twenty-first-century interactivity with the drama. Therefore, until the large entertainment corporations can truly build one of Toffler's simulated environments, the mass-market computer industry will effectively provide the virtual simulated environment through such games as *Myst* and *Riven*.

PART IV

At the Interface: Webpages as Sites of Immersion

Interface Design as Performance: A Link Between Fantasy and Reality

BY TRACY N. SCHMETTERER

Since the 1970s, computer systems and the changes they have undergone have been a dramatic illustration of technological growth. Enormous, noisy machines that were monitored by hand and kept in a chilled room to keep them from overheating were what the world once knew as computers. "The tape drives alone (the equivalent of today's floppy disks) were the size of refrigerators" (Murray 1997:2–3). The demands of the 1990s have transformed these systems into tinier, faster machines that are portable, user-friendly, and extremely accessible. The invention of the World Wide Web has provided much of this accessibility, and the web is now reaching schools and homes all over the world. Web browsers and search engines, such as Netscape and Internet Explorer, make locating reference materials and databases of information fast and simple. The popularity of the internet can mostly be attributed to the creation and expansive use of hypertext. Janet Murray explains that hypertext is "a set of documents (images, texts, charts, tables, video clips) connected to one another by links" (1997:55). These pages of imagery and sound all become available to the viewers through a "homepage" that acts as an introduction to the site they have chosen to explore. It is this page that presents an interface of an interactive website. In addition, perhaps the interface of a website acts as a direct link between fantasy and reality in a performative way, shaping the audience's journey from one to the other through design and media fandom. If this is true, then the *Buffy the Vampire Slayer* website, created by Warner Brothers, provides a creative interface that exemplifies such a performative exploration of a fantasy topic.

The design of the interface of a site is obviously influential in a viewer's experience, but how this design shapes the medium into performance is compelling. Jon McKenzie defines cultural performance as "the embodiment of [certain] social archives, [and the] restoration and transformation of historical forces in living behavior" (1997:31). Theater, music, and storytelling are some examples of cultural performances. An audience member usually experiences these art forms through live performance, or what McKenzie refers to as "living behavior." This author borrows this idea from Schechner, who claims that "restored behavior is the main characteristic of performance" (1985:35). McKenzie uses performance artist Laurie Anderson's website to explain how interface design can present cultural performances.

In the case of *Buffy the Vampire Slayer*, the actual television show acts as the living behavior. Much like Anderson, Warner Brothers supplements this behavior with visuals and text that connect the viewer to the art form through the web's interface instead of the television screen. Anderson's digital *Puppet Motel* option features rooms that connect and form a type of cyberspace environment which the viewer may visit. "All the rooms in *Puppet Motel* function as discrete performance sites where a guest may play language games ... in this interface of cultural and technological performance, the guest is the performer" (McKenzie 1997:43). Although the "Buffy" interface is much simpler and does not involve the refined technology of CD-ROM games, it contains similar characteristics of performance. This *Buffy the Vampire Slayer* site offers chat rooms, exploratory links, and simple databases of information, which are all quite similar to Anderson's creation. For instance, after clicking several icons, Anderson's users may find themselves in a room titled "The Stage." "Here one may check out a map of the U.S. tour, read some promotional material about her CD's ... even browse through Huang's programming script for *Puppet Motel*" (McKenzie 1997:43). Similarly, *Buffy* users may select "The Yearbook," where they can examine photos, character information, and actor biographies for all of the series' cast members. Each separate link on the interface presents a choice of interaction for the viewer, while they all remain connected to the cultural performance of the fantasy world of *Buffy*. Warner Brothers has truly created its own design language, based on the knowledge of the television series, that causes Buffy to perform on "the virtual community that passes through" this site (McKenzie 1997:46).

Regarding her website, Anderson herself is quoted as saying, "It's about creating imaginary worlds that have a special relationship to reality—

worlds in which we can extend, amplify, and enrich our own capabilities to think, feel, and act" (McKenzie 1997:41). Her CD-ROM interface connects the viewer from the reality of her art to a cyberworld she has created in relation to that work. *Buffy the Vampire Slayer*'s website interface is designed to pull viewers from the reality of their own experiences as computer users or fans to the fantasy world of a television show in which they have taken an interest. Although the designers of this website did not create an entirely new cyberworld that represents that of the Slayer, they use dramatic elements to convey the feeling of such a world. The *Buffy* website interface displays a series of objects that represent links. These objects are in two columns on either side of the screen. There are four such icons on the left and right, and two in the center. All of these objects look very realistic, much like photographs, and they are presented against a plain black background. When users move the mouse across any one of these icons, they discover that each object moves and describes, through text, what it represents. For example, a neatly stacked deck of tarot cards is placed as the second icon from the top left column on the interface. When the participant moves the mouse over this icon, white text appears to the right of the cards that states: "Moloch's Revenge: Interactive Game." The card deck also spreads and refolds itself continuously until the mouse moves away from the icon. Detailed visual icons that move act as spectacle, and the interface is directly linked to variations of thought, plot, and character that embody the imaginary environment of *Buffy the Vampire Slayer*. The interface designed for *Buffy* fans truly provides a "theatrical domain" in which they may interact and perform as desired (McKenzie 1997:41). Through careful design, the interface provides references and theatrical elements that allow visitors to connect and interact with a fantasy world they could previously view only on television.

An interface is something that connects the viewer to others while simultaneously providing a personal journey. At the interface, users may realize there are others in the world around them who have similar interests, and most importantly, that these others are anonymous and cannot be categorized. Daniel Mackay speaks extensively about the "existing social and political milieu" in society that has created a gap between everyday life and the artistic (2001:149). The milieu Mackay establishes refers to America's focus on industry and structures of power that support the country's economy. This focus leaves little room for fantasy or art because the imaginative is seen as "non-productive" and "expendable." He describes this further as an "alienation between how the contemporary ideology is embodied in daily life and the idiosyncratic production of the past" (149). This dialectic can be seen in the contrast between non-interactive television and the shared medium of websites. An interface such as *Buffy* inherently bridges this societal gap, allowing viewers to break through the stereotyping sociopolitical norms that isolate the social world from one of fantasy.

It is the very nature of the interface to reconnect people with a shared social experience through an art form. The majority of people visiting the *Buffy* website have a common interest in the television show, and they are immediately relating to one another about something that is completely outside the realm of daily life. In this particular example, Mackay's theories are even more relevant because *Buffy the Vampire Slayer* is based on fantasy. Not only do viewers reconnect with their peers, stripped of the societal milieu that is so disengaging, but they are able to immerse themselves in a world of fantasy totally separate from anything cognizant of the roles they take on in everyday life. The fantasy world of *Buffy* forms a spiritual basis for interaction. However, such interaction is only possible if the design of the interface encourages role-play for its viewers. Role-play supports a fully immersive and interactive use of the interface. More importantly, however, it is role-play that allows the participant to leave his or her societal self behind, in turn leaving behind social burdens.

When the user first approaches the *Buffy* homepage, an entirely black screen is displayed while grayish-purple icons that resemble Gothic tapestries appear to the far right and left of the webpage. These banners provide two options for the visitor (depending on how fast one's modem is), but they are essential in beginning to create an environment that will satisfy the viewer's need for role-play. The color of the banners is similar to the setting of the series. Scenes from the television show often take place in a cemetery or warehouse, and the backgrounds are often gray and in shadows. The *Buffy* series also makes numerous references to centuries past, explaining the origin of many of the vampires and monsters that appear on the show. These banners are simple, but they give viewers the feeling that they are immersed in the environment of *Buffy* immediately. A third icon is slowly displayed directly between these two banners with the same color font, revealing the title *Buffy the Vampire Slayer*, including the statement "Buffy needs your help." The title is wavy and fades slowly in and out of view, creating a mystical atmosphere, while "your" invites the viewer to explore the site in a personal way. The colors and visual effects of this simple preface express an initial sense of the mystical feeling of the television show while giving one an opportunity to participate, almost as if one were a character. This webpage is simply an introduction to the main interface, and it already encourages the viewer to begin a "role-play" as a *Buffy* participant, while invoking a feeling of community. Viewers are aware that they are about to become a part of a fantasy world of Gothic mysticism that others enjoy, and they are personally invited to share in the experience. Users also recognize that once they are connected to the fantasy world, they are no longer simply passive witnesses to performance through a television screen.

The "bestiary" option, which is represented with a monster's skull that opens its jaws when the user passes a mouse across it, leads to a wealth of information about the various demons that have appeared on the show, including bios and photos of all the evil characters of *Buffy*. As viewers move their mouse over each icon, exploring how they might move, they may feel a bit like slayers themselves. Traveling through a screen full of shadows and moving slowly from demons to monsters is similar to how one experiences the television show. The design of this interface allows the viewer to hunt for information in an environment that simulates the one in which Buffy hunts evil. However, others could be simultaneously sharing in the experience of the site while the viewer is creating the journey, whereas the television provides a set performance in which there is no such choice. Although all of this may be temporary, the goal of the interface is to create something from a common interest to be "shared by the players as an alternate reality they all live in together" (Murray 1997:44). The result is the very sense of community expressing an artistic base that Mackay contends society has lost.

Once the viewer passes through the central interface screen, which contains the moving icons referenced earlier, the Warner Brothers designers simply expanded this detailed creation of an imaginary environment. However, Mackay points out that "while the temporary visitor of the imaginary environment wants to believe in it ... he cannot bring himself to permanently believe in a fantasy" (2001:149). It is my belief that this statement is precisely the point. The interface provides a temporary break from feelings of alienation and separates viewers from daily life for brief moments of time. These moments act as a substantial release for the viewer, because the experience of the fantasy world occurs through role-playing. The interface allows the reality of the user, sitting at a computer and moving a mouse, to connect with the visual fantasy provided. Perhaps, the more effective the interface design, the more immersive it may be, no matter how brief.

The designers of a site such as *Buffy the Vampire Slayer* must keep in mind both fans and newcomers to the show while weighing the importance of link options and visual displays. This particular example of an interface personifies how the design of a page can satisfy the needs of all types of visitors. Henry Jenkins describes fans as those "whose cultural preferences and interpretive practices seem so antithetical to dominant aesthetic logic" (1992:19). This viewpoint leads one to conceptualize the fan as the "other," or the fanatic whose life revolves around a specific show or movie. The *Buffy* interface provides assorted visual icons that are ambiguous to everyone observing them, including fans. Even experienced viewers may not be able to conclude where these images lead without actually initiating exploration through clicking — thus making them all the more curious.

Icons such as a monstrous skull and a deck of cards immediately place viewers on the same level, eliminating the dreaded "other." These icons, of course, lead to portions of the site that are more interesting to hardcore fans, and others that are strictly for *Buffy* beginners. However, the main problem of relating to both types of viewers when they initially approach the site has been easily resolved. Newcomers to *Buffy* would find the icons entertaining, while being offered various options that link them to learning more about the show, its characters, actors, and so forth. At the same time, the fan is intrigued and may begin trying to guess the path behind each image, creating a game-like environment that is just as satisfying. In both cases, the participant is linked to a fantasy world in a comfortable way.

Once again, it is television that creates a gap between viewers. Newcomers to *Buffy the Vampire Slayer* may be confused after watching one episode to which fans relate most. It is television that disconnects these two different types of viewers. The icons displayed represent integral pieces of the television show and connect the participant directly to Buffy's world. Jenkins contends that "the meaning of appropriate symbols ... lay not in their inherent meanings but rather in the logic of their use" (1992:39). A website of symbols creates a separate journey for each visitor, depending on how he or she chooses to use them. Moreover, *Buffy the Vampire Slayer*'s interface easily allows viewers to feel as though they are not only exploring the television world, but that they are part of an equal community of people who are just as interested in this environment as they themselves are.

Although it is entertaining for fans to explore sites that deal exclusively with their common interest, a need to have a more direct link to the show presents itself. "Like other popular readers, fans lack direct access to the means of commercial cultural production and have only the most limited resources with which to influence [the] entertainment industry's decisions" (Jenkins 1992:26). When hardcore fans approach the *Buffy* interface, they are introduced to options that immediately gratify this urge for direct contact. From a general perspective, the Warner Brothers site itself acts as a direct link to the industry. More specifically, the interface option that displays a visual image of a theatrical stage along with the description "The Bronze: Chat Posting Board" immediately communicates that the viewer has input into this site. Chat rooms where ideas and opinions can be discussed communicate the possibility that fans' ideas will be reviewed by the people who created the website (the industry itself). Such direct interaction with the commercial part of a show, while actually participating in an entertaining type of role-play, may be attractive to the fan. This opportunity to express opinions and ideas is unthinkable for those dealing singularly with a non-interactive television. The *Buffy* interface allows the knowledgeable viewer to feel connected to the show at this point, even if through a simple visual icon.

Jenkins believes that fans who explore fields of entertainment "in a fashion that serves different interests, [act as] spectators who transform the experience of watching television into a rich and complex participatory culture" (1992:23). Although Jenkins is speaking of fan fiction in this instance, perhaps the creators of a website would completely agree. Warner Brothers created such a site in relation to the popular cult television show *Buffy the Vampire Slayer* with many viewers in mind. Their visual creation transforms the living behavior of this fan following into a performative journey through a computer. Such a journey cannot be provided through television alone. The experience of this interaction gives the audience a chance to feel a part of a larger community, where social distinction is eliminated and where one can connect to the fantasy one may or may not know as a series in an interactive way. Fans and newcomers to *Buffy the Vampire Slayer* are provided with a direct link to a world of fantasy through the interface, while the reality of what they are doing remains secure. Through fandom and design, the internet may be cathartic and highly entertaining, creating its "own culture built from the semiotic raw materials the media provides" (Jenkins 1992:49).

Godzilla Attacks the World Wide Web

BY REBECCA FELDMAN

Barry's Temple of Godzilla, Godzilla's Home Page, Official Godzilla Trivia Quiz, Godzilla Toho Topia, Godzilla 2000, and *Godzilla Monster Gallery* are only a few of the numerous websites dedicated to the infamous and oversized prehistoric creature. The online Godzilla community is huge, encompassing a wealth of information on the giant lizard, and games, chat rooms, online toy stores, and video clips are all just waiting to be discovered. These websites can be viewed as performance because they involve an active relationship between a text or script and the viewer. Without an audience (the viewer), a website would cease to have a purpose. Moreover, when a website is entered, explored, and closed, a performance has occurred. In short, Godzilla is being performed on the internet. As an example of how a Godzilla website is a performance, I will examine in detail *Godzilla.com* and give overviews of *Barry's Temple of Godzilla* and *Ask Godzilla.*

When *Godzilla.com* is entered, the viewer is greeted by the word "Godzilla" in large black letters surrounded by a green mist that wavers as if it were a subatomic cloud. Underneath this in smaller letters are the words "Welcome to the Official Jumpstation of Godzilla." On the left is an image of Godzilla from the American Godzilla movie. She (the creature is actually a mother) is standing in front of the Flatiron Building with her jaws wide open. The image to the right of this is an animated version of Godzilla's head. This Godzilla is a light purple color and again has wide-open jaws.

Godzilla is a registered trademark of Toho Co., Ltd.

The first glimpse of *Godzilla.com* introduces the viewer to what Schechner would describe as drama. By his definition, the actual website *Godzilla.com* is the drama. The physical location and design of the site can be accessed by people who are independent of its purpose (1988:72). Underneath the Godzilla welcome banner, the viewer can scroll down to see a list of areas that can be visited. The website is clearly laid out and easy to navigate. Each area has a title in white letters and a descriptive paragraph in orange block letters. Underneath that is a green "X" with two arrows on either side. Finally, underneath this "X" are the words "click here" in small green letters. The five areas that the user can enter by scrolling down and clicking on the green "X" are as follows: "Godzilla: The Series"; "Godzilla: The Movie"; "Godzilla: The Online Game"; "G-Database"; and the "G-Store."

It can be argued, according to Schechner's definition, that this list of possible areas to access is the script of the website, or rather "the basic code of events" (1988:72). In a traditional performance — for example, a three-act play — a script is transmitted from person to person via performers who can instruct the others about the script. In the instance of *Godzilla.com*, the script is transmitted by a website that is controlled by a webmaster as well as by the viewer who enacts it. Thus, by engaging in the website, viewers actively take part in conveying the information about Godzilla to themselves. Therefore, when viewers begin to explore the specific areas of this website, a kind of theater has been entered. Schechner defines theater as "the event enacted by a specific group of performers" (1988:72).

The first area to visit is "Godzilla: The Series." This is an animation adventure series that takes up where the last Godzilla movie ended. When you first arrive in this area you see a cartoon version of Godzilla clutching the Chrysler Building. This image is surrounded by a cartoon rendering of the panels of an Atari-like videogame control board. On the left are options in thick black lettering — "The Show," "The Cast," "Heat Team," and "Godzilla" — which provide detailed descriptions of the animated series.

Upon entering "Godzilla: The Movie," the viewer sees the Godzilla logo once again with a green image of the creature on a green and black graph that says "Guess Who's Here." To the left are three spinning neon-green radar screens. Scrolling down reveals eighteen areas to access, all having to do with the film *Godzilla* (1998). They state the date that the information was added, and range from games to chat rooms and informational segments. All of these links allow the viewer to enter another part of the "theater." The next area, "Godzilla: The Online Game," reveals a large red spiral with the words "Take to the Streets in a Monster Battle" in orange letters on the screen. On the bottom right is a round shape that alternately flashes "Play" with an image of Godzilla's eyeball. Clicking this produces a screen inviting one to register as a character and join the online Godzilla community. After this is completed, the viewer can click an icon and begin interactive play. There are also links to other online games, such as *Air Warrior, Air Warrior Three, Aliens Online, Claw, Game Blasts, Battletech, Splatterball, Starship Troopers, Stellar Explorer,* and *Warcraft.*

The visitor can continue to explore and interact in the next two sections as well. In "G-Database," a black screen with a red top appears. In large black letters at the top of the screen the words "Godzilla Classic" appear, surrounded by Japanese letters. Underneath this is an image of four Japanese Godzillas breathing fire. They are surrounded by Japanese characters and terrified people. Around this picture are yellow dots that say "GO," signifying entry to the database. When one clicks on one, a gigantic list of everything having to do with Godzilla appears. This huge database allows the viewer to locate information divided into the categories of movie, monster, and director. For example, clicking on *Godzilla vs. The Smog Monster* under the heading "movie" brings up a comprehensive five-page entry on this movie. Finally, the last option on the menu is the "G-Store." Upon entering, the visitor is presented with a black, blue, and gray screen with images of such items as action figures, clothing, towels, and posters. Clicking on an item links the visitor to a screen stating prices and order information.

Another Godzilla website that is an example of a Godzilla performance on the internet is *Barry's Temple of Godzilla.* The first image in the performance of this site is of a giant green foot that moves slowly up and down next to the words "Barry's Temple of Godzilla" in large red letters. To the left is a list of twenty-five areas to access, which include "New Information," "Video Clips," "Film Clips," and "Photo Gallery." Upon entering the Photo Gallery, the title appears at the top of the screen in bold black letters, and at the bottom are three black boxes superimposed over a background of blue, gray, and yellow caution signs. The three boxes are labeled "Godzilla," "Original Art Gallery," and "The Ghidorah Gallery." Underneath these boxes are a line of cartoon baby Godzilla images. If the Godzilla Gallery is chosen, a screen with eleven rows of photos of Godzilla from various films appears. If one of these photos is chosen, the photo comes up full-screen size.

Ask Godzilla is a website geared toward children who have questions about Godzilla. The first glimpse of this site shows a black screen with neon-green type that says in large lettering, "Guess Who's Coming to

Town?" Underneath in smaller letters are the words "Ask Godzilla." There is a paragraph that offers a description of the site, together with a section that includes questions sent by e-mail, along with answers. Some of the questions include: What does Godzilla eat? Who is Godzilla's best friend? and How much does Godzilla weigh?

The performance of Godzilla through the internet on these sites is achieved through the wide variety and vast number of websites that can be accessed and interacted with, immersing fans into a large Godzilla culture. Whether websites allow people to learn more about the background history of Godzilla or simply to order a new toy online, these websites become a liminal environment where visitors can exit the everyday world for a time and enter a place of fantasy.

Mulder and Scully Together at Last: The Feminine Demonstration of Scully in Fan Art on the Web

BY STEPHANIE DALQUIST

Many websites include fan fiction, in which fans of their favorite television show, movies, books, or even comic books produce creative works set in another's fantasy universe. These works can exist in media as diverse as prose, painting, animation, music, and even film. They offer a new kind performance into the universe, and many of them contain alternative interpretations and histories that tend to reflect the desires of the fans. In fan fiction, fans control the performance. Chris Carter's *The X-Files*, originally set in a television series running since 1993, is one particular environment that has inspired a great many authors of fan fiction. The two lead characters, FBI agents Fox Mulder and Dana Scully, work to explain X-Files, cases involving paranormal or alien phenomena. These characters have always existed in an environment of sexual tension, prompting the creative involvement of devoted fans who create further story lines in various media.

In looking at any sort of fan fiction, it is necessary to explore the author's motivations and method of writing within that universe. Fan stories of *The X-Files* usually fall into the context of emotional intensification bordering on eroticization, which in itself frequently involves a genre shift to the generic model of romance, as explained by media-fan scholar Henry Jenkins (see Jenkins 1992:174). This fiction is largely written by and for the (surprisingly large) female demographic which is interested in the show. The subject, then, not only reflects upon the gender role of woman as sensitive nurturer and emotional being, but allows the characteristic "chick flick" emotional topics to enter into *The X-Files* environment, albeit in the artistic works of fans rather than in the original television medium. This explains not only the surprising number of emotional topics in *The X-Files* fan fiction, but also the recurring theme of the exploration of Scully's feminine side, which is largely suppressed throughout most of the series. Tension between the fan desire for this exploration and the producers' unwillingness to deliver a romantic encounter between Mulder and Scully forces the fans to fulfill their desires within these other media. Fan art images allow the artists to perform fantasies of Mulder and Scully having a romantic relationship, a relationship that some fans want to see on the show.

Thus, the specific interests guiding *The X-Files* fan fiction are provoked by the sexual tension between Mulder and Scully that has existed since the series began in 1993. Fans have been clamoring for a romantic entanglement between the two, and have been repeatedly teased by almost-kiss scenes and an occasional romance between one true character and one who is represented by a shape-shifter. Such tantalization has only instigated more fiction along these lines, including the two art-work images created through computer-altered graphics, illustrating fan artists' depiction of an idealized romantic fantasy between Mulder and Scully. Reading these images like a text, it can be argued that the theme of these two creations I examine below reveals Scully's femininity—not as a reduction of her professional role as an FBI agent, but as a projected fantasy "demonstrating" a feminine aspect of Scully never shown on the television series.

Daydream—image located at *www.ciudadfutura.com/expedientex/daydream.jpg*

In the fan image "Daydream," we find a sexual reading of Scully's character as she thinks about Mulder while lying in bed. This picture reveals a medium shot of Scully lying on her back on a white-sheeted bed with a half-faded close-up picture of Mulder (in his suit and tie) above her body, like a daydream image. An interesting point about the overall scope of this picture is that Mulder and Scully are not *physically together* as they are often depicted in other fan photos. The author has successfully captured not only the assumed desire of Scully to be with Mulder, but also her own fantasy of having Scully be with Mulder, and indeed, in all likelihood, her fantasy of *herself* dreaming about Mulder/David Duchovny. This sort of metatextual analysis begins to reveal the image as a multilayered exhibit, a cultural performance containing a deep structure and cultural significance.

First of all, Scully is depicted as a sexual and feminine being, instead of Agent Scully as we see her on the series. Depending on the interpreters' point of view, she could be "reduced to" this state or "demonstrated in" it. The choice of "reduced to" would imply an inferiority of the feminine self to the professional self. The creator of the image is unlikely to have put a favorite character into an inferior position within the context of her graphical fan fiction, because what distinguishes this creator is her desire to see the characters satiate their desire and pursue a romantic relationship. Her intent to create this reality through her artwork implies that the relationship is as valued or more valued than the professional relationship exhibited in the series. So, rather than implying that her femininity is reductive or negative, it is likely that Scully is being *demonstrated* or *performed* as female, again reflecting the typical desires of the author and other fan fiction viewers exploring the nonprofessional side of their favorite character.

The evidence for this performance lies all about the image. Obviously, the subject of her daydream and the physical locale in which she is having it have a sexual connotation. Everything in Scully's environment is white, a far cry from the dark, austere suits portraying her professionally. White also symbolizes, in a larger cultural context, purity, hope, light, good, and other abstract phenomena, which lead to a generalized classification of feminine. The sheets and blankets are white as well and have a slightly rumpled effect which, combined with the lighting from the right side of the picture, suggests a light rippling, a softness, in contrast to a freshly made bed with sheets stretched flat. Add to this the *soft* focus of the shot, and this mixture designates the femininity of Dana Scully in bed. Even the title, "Daydream," connotes a more innocent fantasy of ladylike demeanor, as opposed to a vivid sexual fantasy that could have been as easily created.

Scully's fantasy cannot be left alone as just another daydream, however. First, although created by a woman, it reconfirms the culturally imposed stereotype that women are always thinking about men. Not only is she thinking about men, she is thinking of a specific man — her FBI partner. This depiction shows her turning, in her mind, a professional relationship into aspirations for romantic involvement. Interestingly, the artist performs Mulder as the consummate suit-and-tie professional that he is by day. Granted that this may have been due to the author's lack of Photoshop skills or available shots of Duchovny, she is not even *imagining* herself with him. His daytime attire brings to mind sociobiological arguments for women wanting men as providers, not lovers—an ideal that ardent fans should complain about, since it is against Scully's nature. The white sheets bear some further exploration here. They do indeed connote feminine traits in both color and texture in contrast with Mulder's dark suit. His professional attire, the contrast between his suit and Scully wrapped only in sheets, emphasizes the otherness and separation of the spheres they inhabit.

The desire for romance and the sexual strength of the image is intensified by the subtle placement of (what appears to be) her hand on her breast. The actuality of that image being her hand and not a bra or elbow is *irrelevant* once it has left the author's hands. The mere *suggestion* that she is touching herself in conjunction with the daydream heightens the performed sexuality of the image and the expression of romantic desire that it conveys. Her facial expression with eyes closed and head tilted gently up in a coy, pleased expression again suggests an implication of her sexuality and the femininity described above.

Every aspect of the shot contributes to the fantastical ambiance of the image. The soft-focus photography not only serves to disguise the true identity of the woman, but it is an element frequently used to create a chimerical or whimsical image because the softening of edges produces a dreamlike effect. The author of the image has also gone to some trouble to add camera flare sunspots to the image in several locations. Several concentric circular glares are located toward the center of the image, to the lower left of her body. They seem to glow like crystals or baubles right out of any fantasy or romance text. Another one is placed directly above her head and glows radiantly, eliciting images of halos and tiaras, commonplace items within the fantasy genre. The wiry bed frame that knots the horizontal wires to the vertical wires is shown only in silhouette, their outline suggesting perhaps tall palms. The rippling effect of the bedding, which contributes to the soft femininity of the room, almost borders the "trunks" of these trees, creating an illusion of waves lapping at the shore. The juxtaposition of the bright sunspot against what would be the horizon adds to the paradisiacal landscape illusion. Of course, such perfect landscapes exist only in one's imagination — and are played out in performances such as this one.

The whole picture is a fantasy. Beyond the fact that it is an imaginary environment, and beyond Scully's daydream, it is still a fantasy shot, reflecting the fantasy of many fans to bring Mulder and Scully together and lusting for one another. It at least reflects the fantasy, (day)dreams, and desire of the author of this image. The author may indeed have participated in the ultimate fantasy here: the woman lying in the bed bears a passing resemblance to Gillian Anderson (Scully), but some argue that it is the artist herself who is in the picture. The viewer is only led to believe that this is Scully by an approximate profile and a shock of red hair reflecting the light outside the viewing angle. The wonderful trick of soft focus blurs the woman's silhouette just enough that the resemblance is uncanny, and once Mulder's face is recognized, the woman in bed is immediately seen as Scully. If the artist has planted herself within this image, the fan has *become* Scully within this text, a variation of the "Mary Sue" stories. This genre of fan fiction allows the author entrance into the imaginary environment to "efface the gap that separates the realm of their own experience and the fictional space of their favorite programs" (Jenkins 1992:171). Instead of casting herself as a rookie agent or other co-star, as is done in most Mary Sue stories, this artist has visually, in a concrete way, supplanted herself into the performance of the main role.

Wedding— image found at *www.ciudadfutura.com/expedientex/wedding. htm*

In contrast to "Daydream," "Wedding" takes Scully's relationship with her partner, Mulder, beyond a dream to a permanent commitment, which maintains a more conservative femininity of Scully. A sepia-colored picture reveals Scully in a wedding gown with Mulder standing next to her, holding her arm. On the left side of the picture is text, written as a wedding invitation. As a cultural text, this picture naturally extends past the point at which "Daydream" left off. Representation of a wedding indicates a romantic relationship that has progressed beyond mere daydreams. The key difference is that this image brings Mulder and Scully out of the universe in which they were created and into our own world. It invites the viewer to join this fantasy.

Whereas "Daydream" brought the artist into Mulder and Scully's world, "Wedding" brings them out of the imaginary entertainment environment and into our real world. The text of the invitation reads, "Dana Katherine Scully and Fox William Mulder request the pleasure of your company as they are united in matrimony on Friday, the nineteenth of June nineteen hundred and ninety-eight at three o' clock in the afternoon. The Embassy Park Plaza Hotel District of Columbia." Washington, DC, has always been a key setting for the television show. It appears on the invitation as a component signifying that it is just as important to the wedding as it is to those who will be married. The realism of the image is furthered by the use of the Embassy Park Plaza, a real hotel, as the site of the wedding. The viewer connects the hotel with the background setting of the invitation picture, such that the city and the hotel come to life as key actors in the wedding. What makes this so real is the view we have of the locale — a fancy hotel-like background occupies more than half of the picture, bringing it to life in our reality. It is further separated from the typical *X-Files* environment by the decor. *The X-Files* occurs in some unusual and diverse locales, but the gilded hotel look is not among them. The event itself extricates itself from Mulder and Scully's environment. Just as the setting shown does not occur in the show, neither do weddings — it is science fiction, not a soap opera or harlequin romance.

The photographic technique can also be compared to that used in "Daydream," the contrast between the two further exemplifying how "Wedding" has been brought into the real world. Most noticeably, the sepia tone of the photograph is rarely used in the context of television. It evokes a reality and history that are inconsistent with the modernity of television in general and of this series in particular. This is in stark opposition to the whites and light grays present in "Daydream." The lack of special effects brings this image even closer to our reality. The soft focus and sunspots that defined the dreamlike qualities of the first image are absent here, anchoring the event even more firmly within reality.

On the one hand, as described above, the characters are brought into our world to be "united in matrimony." On the other hand, the viewer of the image is being invited into their world. The careful wording of the invitation and the body language of the people in the picture communicate this. It is stated most directly in the invitation, that the "pleasure of *your* company is requested." The invitation is directly addressed to the viewer of the image, pulling the viewer into its performance. The viewer is not simply asked to watch, but is named as "company," implying interaction between the characters within this universe and us, the viewer. This invites the viewer to partake in a visual "Mary Sue" fan fiction story, entering the characters' universe to watch and participate in the moments that bring this mythical relationship to the next level. Scully herself seems to be beckoning the viewer to enter her world with a direct gaze. Her eyes are shadowed in such a way that her gaze seems to call the viewer from any angle that the picture is viewed, a persuasive gesture, summoning the viewer into the imaginary environment. Her right hand is placed gently over the dress where her hip or upper leg would fall, as if having just tapped it to coax the viewer forward, into her universe.

The recurring theme in this image and in "Daydream" is the consideration of Scully's femininity, as compared to the professional persona that has been carefully developed in the television series. The femininity described by this image performs a more traditional femininity than shown in "Daydream." Scully here is a more conservative, much less sexual being than was shown in the other image. As with the first image, the differences are emphasized in dress and posture. Mulder, at his own wedding, is not even wearing a tuxedo. He is dressed in the same sort of suit he wears for every episode, resulting in a lack of differentiation between Mulder's at-work personality and Mulder at home. This lack of differentiation also occurs in "Daydream." Scully, in contrast, is not in the sensible suit she wears when working with Mulder, but is wearing an ultra-feminine wedding gown. The curves emphasize her chest and feminine form. The wide skirts remind the viewer that this is a *dress* on a *woman*. Indirectly, it becomes a performance of her sexuality — the placement of her hand on her hip, for example, brings to mind childbearing, and this interpretation is strengthened by the shadowy formation of a stomach above her arm.

For the same reasons as considered for "Daydream," it is unlikely that the artist intends to demean Scully's character by portraying her as feminine. Any fan invested enough in an imaginary environment to create fan fiction around it, as stated earlier, is not motivated by the idea of depicting the characters in a defamatory situation. The more traditional setup, characterized by the sepia tones of the photograph and by Scully's costume, implies a more conservative take on femininity. In this case, the author has not put herself physically into the picture, but has performed her values in the image by manifesting her ideals on Scully's nonprofessional traits. The same contrast of dark and light in costume that was seen in "Daydream" is also seen here. Scully's white dress is uncharacteristic of her as she has been developed in the television series. A conventional cut for a wedding dress, with a long gown and tight bodice, again emphasizes the separate spheres that the author envisions Mulder and Scully inhabiting. The sepia tone works here again by suggesting the nostalgia for the conservative femininity that has since been culturally encoded as a standard at the time sepia tone was popularly used in photographs.

Conclusion — These images are only two of many that reveal fans' relationships with *The X-Files*, one of many imaginary entertainment environments in which fans participate. Fan authors and artists contribute to the history and culture of *The X-Files* by creating works published on the World Wide Web. Fans are not just consumers of culture, they are participants of it. Here, a fan contributed to the development of Scully's femininity, which is virtually untouched during the regular television series. Despite the fact that the romantic narratives depicted in these images may never appear on the television series, the fans' work extends the history of these characters beyond the producers' television series and reveals that the show really belongs to the viewers, the fans of *The X-Files*, for they are the ones who will continue to create new narratives when the television series eventually ends.

Immersion Through an Interface in The Blair Witch Project

BY KURT LANCASTER

The Blair Witch Project's website (located at *http://www.blairwitch.com*) was created in 1998 to advertise the then forthcoming 1999 film. Tropes from the film, even before it was shown in movie houses, were embedded on this website, allowing participants to reexperience them later at the movies. Others saw the film first, then reexperienced the film on the website. In a sense, the participants become virtual performers on a kind of computer stage.

On the opening page, the real filmmakers set up a teaser — an attention-grabbing incident — that intrigued the potential spectator-participants. On a black background in white lettering, the page read: "In October of 1994, three student filmmakers disappeared into the woods near Burkittsville, Maryland, while shooting a documentary. A year later their footage was found." Many people, including a person who called in to the Howard Stern radio show, believed this trope to be real. At the roots of this teaser is a code of horror that intrigues the reader. October is the month of Halloween, the night when legend and myth describe fairies and witches crossing from an unseen spirit world to haunt the lives of mortals — who in this case are the fictional filmmakers attempting to document on film what cannot be seen: the legend, spirit, and power of a metaphysical haunting. As for all who attempt to quantify the unknown and the mysterious, the attempt fails, and the filmmakers disappear in a forest, a mythical symbol that houses dark and foreboding fears, from which nothing can escape. Burkittsville, Maryland, conveys a sense of horror lurking in an inhabited land — a suburb in Maryland — unlike the horrors contained in a wilderness when the first settlers came from the Old World to the new. Within this civilization are the tools of science that discover the "lost" footage which contains a lurking mystery that can only be answered by entering the website designed to bring about a kind of investigative/scientific performance through the use of an interface.

The interface makes concrete the imaginary. It is the mediating object by which we are enticed into an imaginary world — by which we perceive an imaginary person, place, or thing. How the interface is designed determines how we experience the imaginary in the physical, phenomenological world. The interface determines how we interact and perceive the content. Many people tend to think about the kinds of interfaces computers have. But computers are not the only place we encounter interfaces. Anytime we view a work of art, visit a theater, or see a movie, we are confronted with an interface. For example, if we are going to read Shakespeare's *Henry V* we will experience the content of that play differently than if we watched Kenneth Branagh's 1989 film production. The production makes concrete the play which we may have only previously "viewed" through our imagination in the theater of the mind when read. A play is an interface into an author's imaginary environment. Performers rehearse at "living" in this milieu. Their behavior, as well as the lights, sound, and costumes comprising the mise-en-scène, represents a physicalization of the author's imaginary world of the play. The audience perceives the author's imaginary construct through the interface of the mise-en-scène onstage.

The *Star Wars* computer games *Jedi Knight* and *X-Wing*, on the other hand, offer a different kind of interface design, allowing the participant to enter George Lucas's imaginary universe from different perspectives. A film such as *Star Wars* or *The Blair Witch Project* requires a 35-mm film projector and a movie house (or videotape, VCR, and television). Computer games require a computer and joystick. In the former we participate in the universe as spectators. In the latter we participate as performers in Lucas's imaginary environment. In the computer game *Jedi Knight* we are given a first-person view by which we can shoot up storm troopers and duel alien beings with a lightsaber. In *X-Wing* we fly a first-person view of various fighter ships from the movies, shooting up Imperial Tie-Fighters and cruisers. The joystick and onscreen data become the interface — the concrete material object — by which we experience Lucas's fantasy universe: a universe first experienced on a movie screen — the result of the concrete physicalization of Lucas's imagination. Through various interface objects—from actors to set designs and film technologies—he is able to share that imagination with others.

Similarly, the *Blair Witch* site presents a different kind of interface in order to evoke its mise-en-scène on a digital stage, which requires a different kind of interface to experience than that of a conventionally staged drama or an action-oriented video game. The *Blair Witch* site requires the click of a mouse to navigate through its drama "onstage." In this site, one would assume that the various links presented on a menu page—"Mythology," "The Filmmakers," "The Aftermath," and "The Legacy"—would take the viewer to pages describing the background information on the film: the real filmmakers' initial concept, story treatments, how they made the film, and their legacy as now legendary filmmakers. Instead, the viewer gets further information that make the fantasy seem even more real, placing the viewer more deeply into the drama. Also on the menu page, the witchcraft image of the Blair Witch—comprising part of the mise-en-scène—lures the participant into its intriguing horror, a crucifix-like symbol: a cross on which a figure hangs with legs outstretched. It is an artifact of mystery and a seal of doom foreshadowing the horror and death of the filmmakers—an experience that the spectator can experience vicariously. Just click the mouse, and participants will be taken to this world of horror, scene by scene, immersing them into its thought-provoking multimedia horror.

For example, under the link "Mythology" the user finds these pages containing specific dates from February 1785 to December 15, 1995, documenting the various events that start with an entry presenting an illusion of historical accuracy of witchcraft in American culture: February, 1785: "Several children accuse Elly Kedward of luring them into her home to draw blood from them. Kedward is found guilty of witchcraft, banished from the village during a particularly harsh winter and presumed dead." The final entry describes how the *Blair Witch Project* documentary footage was turned over to the parents of the victims, who, in turn, gave it to a film company to edit together. And this presumably becomes the film released in movie theaters.

The tropes of horror—such as the textual image of disembowelment under the March 1886 entry—further the design of the webpage creators to seduce the participant into discovering the resolution of such horror, what Marshall Blonsky calls "the last stand of hell in America," which "takes place in the closet of simulated catharsis," perhaps slightly cleansed from "our nightmares," but "not driven to action" (1992:370–371).

At the same time, the seduction of realism contained within this site's mise-en-scène evokes a pattern similar to the one presented in Orson

Welles's radio production of *The War of the Worlds* on October 30, 1938. What made the radio production so striking was how Welles combined the radio interface with the use of realistic news broadcasts. By wedding the fictional radio story with the news broadcast, Welles tapped into and manipulated an existing social and cultural understanding: that radio news is a reliable source of information. By doing so, he was able to take a fictional story and make it appear *as if* real — at least to those who did not tune in to the beginning of the broadcast and failed to hear the disclaimer that the broadcast was a work of fiction. According to a Princeton University study, over one million people (about 10 percent of the listeners) believed the broadcast was real and were frightened by it (cited in Clute and Nichols 1995:1300).

The *Blair Witch* site seems to evoke a similar horror of a power beyond one's control. Can such horror exist? The website beckons its siren lure, blurring the foundation of reality with a realistically presented fantasy. Roland Barthes believes that various social and cultural codes embedded within literature tend to manipulate the participant's view of reality. In fact, Barthes contends that all literature — whether in books, online, on film, or in advertising — contains inherent codes that shape or manipulate some aspect of reality: "Everything happens as if the picture *naturally* conjured up the concept, as if the signifier [the image] *gave a foundation* to the signified [the concept]" (1972:129–130). This process Barthes calls the creation of a mythology: the concept becomes the dominant ideology, which is born when specific ideas are used to manipulate images. Some could call this a mesmeric influence manipulating us. So, we must decipher these codes in order to see how the idea manipulates our sense of reality.

Like Welles, the creators of the *Blair Witch Project* website use existing cultural and social codes to manipulate the participant into thinking that there is perhaps some truth to the legend of the Blair Witch. These include the use of such realistic codes as documentary evidence, scientific and archeological findings, historical legend of witchcraft, and, perhaps most importantly, a culture of pseudo-realism promoted by "real TV" which feeds a hungry public starving for something extraordinary to occur in their otherwise mundane lives. All of this information becomes stored in the cultural psyche, and it activates the imagination when people enter the website and see the film. When this occurs, the strips of embedded behavior come alive (activated by the participant engaging the interface). Theater director and performance theorist Richard Schechner, in his theory of restored behaviors, posits that performers can treat "living behavior as a film director treats a strip of film. These strips of behavior can be rearranged or reconstructed.... They have a life of their own" (1985:35). In the *Star Wars* computer games, for example, strips of behavior are borrowed from the films, placed in a new context — into a different interface — and the spectator now reexperiences or re-performs the films as a performer in the *Star Wars* universe. This occurs when participants recognize and identify certain cultural tropes or "codes" that fire their imagination in a new way. The interface object allows the strips of stored behavior contained in the interface to transmit the imaginary and cultural environment to them and through them. Thus spectators become performers.

And thus we click the mouse in an attempt, perhaps, to resolve the Blair Witch horror into answers that will cleanse our minds of Columbine School shootings. Our action turns inward, the guns keep racking up, and we are led to a mythical horror, one from the spirit world without need of such weapons. Clicking on "Heather's Journal," we are led to the inner thoughts of the fictional director of *The Blair Witch Project*, the documentary that would, perhaps, make her career.

Onscreen, we see Heather's old weather-beaten journal right down to water stains and blurred handwriting. The use of science-like analysis tends to make the journal appear real and furthers the plausibility of the story. Since the journal is "All-Weather," we can believe that it could endure the elements for years, waiting to be discovered and read. Heather's journal is like an innocent schoolgirl's, with her name written above an image of pleasant mountains and a rising or setting sun. Inside, we expect to see a journal depicting the physical beauty of a traveler's hike through the woods and mountains of America, the heart of a college student, beyond which we find the solemnity of a setting sun: a symbol of epiphany, of truth lighting the way. Eager to find these truths, we open the pages and find the blue-ink scrawl not of girlish innocence, but a writing revealing clichés and a gender-correct woman of attitude: "Too loud walkman already irritating me.... It seems beggars can't be choosers."

Inside these pages is the truth of a woman making her way in the world as a filmmaker. It tugs the heartstrings and causes us to perhaps pity her. We identify with such a figure of American innocence and promise, to be cut down through old-world horror. "How much to tell the boys?" questions one of the final entries on page 2, dated October 15, 1994. Is this gender empowerment gained from the withholding of a young woman's secrets? The secret, the mystery, impels us to look deeper, page by page, hypertextually weaving ourselves through the linked mise-en-scènes, getting as lost as the filmmakers in the forest of the *Blair Witch*.

Photographs of the 16-mm film cans and ten Hi8-mm tapes "found

by students from the University of Maryland's Anthropology Department"
establish another scientific trope or code to the viewer, restoring certain
previously seen (fictional or not) scientific behaviors that perhaps make
some wonder if this event was indeed real. Evidence on hand causes a belief
in the idea behind the image of that evidence, as Orson Welles learned so
well in his *War of the Worlds* broadcast by simulating the reality of a
reporter's news broadcast. Participants wend themselves through the mise-
en-scène of this site, collecting and bearing witness to the evidence that
makes the event seemingly indisputable.

Pictures of the police's discovery of the filmmaker's car shows what
was never seen in the film. Police photographs, taken in a certain manner, posit a reality based on evidence. At the very least, it extends the film's
performance beyond the movie house and attempts to fulfill the ending
of an otherwise non-ender of the film, in which the witch has killed all of
the student filmmakers. This image embedded in the site activates a clo-
sure that police do exist, that civilization outside the forest still operates
with scientific exactness. Click-click ... click-click ... click-click ... click-
click ... the camera records another abandoned vehicle, a material object
easily captured on film, unlike the spirit of the Blair Witch. Indeed, it only
exists by means of the effect of its imagination on the viewer. The horror
is localized to consciousness. The real filmmakers want the horror to
become activated when we go into the woods.

There is a picture of "the filmmakers," who look like any college students hanging out on campus. We are led to believe that the casual photograph of the three filmmakers was the last time they were seen alive.
This is not the image of the dead, however, as is obvious. Actors portraying roles are so commonplace that some people, when inflicted with a mysterious *idea*, begin to believe the imaginary idea more than the real fact.
Most people knew that the film was fiction, so the webpages created viewer
hype and background information — bits of potential behaviors containing inherent cultural and social codes— that could only be assuaged by
viewing the film itself, pointing back to the website, restoring and re-performing in the minds of these viewers the information embedded within
it. Millions of dollars were made from this film, not because of high production values and amazing special effects of a Hollywood film, for it lacked
all but a budget under $100,000 and had no special effects. Instead, audi-
ences revved by word-of-mouth hype went to reexperience the memories
played out on the website, and, most of all, they went to experience a form
of otherworldly horror, a promise and fear of something out there beyond
the everyday working world of people's mundane lives. They wanted to
experience emotions that, for much of "normal" life, cannot be expressed.

The fictional filmmakers' tears and streaks of terror become our own, not because the history is real, but because they are not real, but simulated. Through immersion by means of an interface we become the performers of a safe horror experience, by which we can become temporarily purged of our own fears, but not cleansed of our mundane lives.

PART V

Interactive Movies

"Let's Do the Time Warp Again": The Survival of The Rocky Horror Picture Show

BY LAUREN KERCHNER

Throughout the history of pop culture, cult following has existed in every entertainment medium from books to movies to music. Thousands of hippies and 1990s neo-hippies worship bands like the Grateful Dead and Phish, following them devotedly from concert to concert; preteens all over the country breathlessly await the release of the latest *Babysitters Club* book series title, while Trekkies convene in droves to pay homage to the classic cult television series, *Star Trek*. Enthusiasm in cult worship is represented in degrees varying from infatuation to near-religious devotion to a chosen medium. When large groups of people form a cult following, they naturally evolve into their own subculture in society that bases itself in the object of the cult's affection. But what makes a cult phenomenon? In his book *Comparative Youth Culture* (1985), Michael Brake speculates that "cults provide meaning, direction, security and a purpose in life for those who found such things lacking in the wider society" (190). By engaging in cult worship, people take on an identity much in the manner of actors assuming roles in a play, giving them an outlet for the release of the personality within them that they may not be able to show in everyday society.

Picture this: it is midnight on a Saturday, and you decide to catch the movie playing at the local multiplex. You buy your ticket and enter the theater, popcorn in hand, anxious to get some firsthand information on this *Rocky Horror Picture Show* flick you have been hearing about. Suddenly, you find yourself in the middle of a party, as the audience around you cheers and hollers while a song-and-dance floor show occurs at the front of the theater. Finally, the lights dim and the picture begins. But instead of obeying the old "Silence is golden" rule, the audience, in an almost chantlike unison, yells out, "and God said, let there be lips!" as a giant pair of red lips appears on the screen to sing "Science Fiction Double Feature" in a voice neither male nor female, setting the androgynous tone for the rest of the phenomenon unraveling itself before you (see Tal). As the film progresses, you find yourself being pelted with rice, squirted with water, and serenaded by live, costumed incarnations of the aliens, scientific creations, and campy transvestites strutting on the screen, finding it more and more difficult to discern which is more important — the theatric pandemonium of the film itself or the theatric pandemonium created by the audience, who respond to nearly every line in the movie with a script all their own. Leaving the theater, you know that you have been a part of a "spectacular happening" — a live performance intertwining itself with a recorded performance to the extent that the two seem inseparable (see Piro). You have taken part in a cult phenomenon, one of pop culture's most famed occurrences in the latter twentieth century.

The phenomenon you witnessed is the ritual of what is perhaps the most unique of all cult groups — the followers of *The Rocky Horror Picture Show*. This 1975 theatrical rock musical turned motion picture has spawned a following unlike that of any other movie: its audience is an integral part of it. A critically discredited film, considered a flop in its first-time big-screen release, *Rocky Horror* was relegated to the position of a "midnight movie." In that position it found its audience, and, perhaps, the missing element to its performance. Unlike other "cult films," *Rocky Horror* fans not only "worship" the movie, they become a part of it by performing together with the characters on the screen.

But why has this campy send-up to science fiction and horror films become one of the most famous cult films of all time? How has it endured for more than twenty years, becoming the timeless cult classic that it is? The answer lies in performance. It is due to its theatrical spectacle, audience participation, and society's need to express itself that *The Rocky Horror Picture Show* has become a cult phenomenon, an undying icon of pop culture spanning a quarter of a century.

In order to understand the evolution of *Rocky Horror* into the experience that it is today, it is first necessary to know its history. The brainchild of actor/musician Richard O'Brien, *Rocky* started out as *The Rocky Horror Show*, a stage musical that premiered in London in 1973 and later moved to the United States, taking the stage in New York City. A theatrical hit, it detailed the wacky story of nerdy, newly engaged Brad Majors and Janet Weiss falling into the hands of the crazy, cross-dressing Transylvanian scientist Dr. Frank N. Furter, his band of cohorts from the planet Transsexual, and his beefcake creation, Rocky Horror, and was soon made into a major motion picture. Produced by Lou Adler and Michael White for 20th Century–Fox, the movie made its American premiere in September 1975 at the Westwood Theater in Los Angeles to poor reviews. After appearing only in test cities, it was considered a failure and shelved, never obtaining widespread release (see Piro).

In April 1976, Tim Deegan, an ad executive for 20th Century–Fox, convinced Bill Quigley of the Walter Reade Organization to replace the midnight show at the Waverly movie theater in New York with *The Rocky Horror Picture Show*, hoping that the midnight crowd might embrace the film's campiness. Over several weeks in the midnight slot, *Rocky Horror*'s audience gained a group of regulars who returned for the growing "party atmosphere" in the theater, which included the playing of music from the movie before the show as a warm-up (see Piro). During the film, audience members increasingly responded with cheers or boos. One night over Labor Day weekend of 1976, an audience member yelled out, "Buy an umbrella, you cheap bitch!" to the onscreen Janet, who covers her head with a newspaper during a rainstorm. Thus began *Rocky Horror*'s audience participation. Credited with this first retort at the screen is Louis Farese, an early regular at the Waverly midnight show. He was quickly followed by many others, who created a myriad of vocal responses to the movie's script. Many of the response lines were repeated at each subsequent viewing of *Rocky*, making them part of the spectator response script that continues to be heard today (see Piro).

Vocal participation was only the first part of the audience contribution to *Rocky Horror*. In April 1977 the use of props in response to the film was introduced when an audience member threw rice at the screen during the wedding scene at the beginning of the film, inspiring others to create props for moments throughout the movie. For instance, in a song sung by Dr. Frank N. Furter (Tim Curry), playing cards were thrown at the screen in response to Frank's line "cards for sorrow, cards for pain." The rainstorm scene in which Janet and Brad find their way to Frank's castle singing, "There's a light over at the Frankenstein Place," provoked audience members to squirt water pistols to simulate the rain, mimic Janet's use of a newspaper as protection, and wave burning candles for the "light." Though the candles, over time, were replaced by flashlights due to movie theater fire-hazard codes, these prop responses became permanent additions to the growing participation in the film.

Halloween marked the beginning of a tradition of audience members dressing up as characters from the film. In doing so, the costumed individuals not only looked like their screen counterparts, but began to assume their roles in the picture by lip-synching or acting out what their chosen characters were doing onscreen. Most popular was doing the "Time Warp"— the dance described in one of the film's most popular songs of the same title. These activities began the tradition of the *Rocky Horror* floor show. One of the fans credited with creating the floor show is Dori Hartley, who led the costume/performance craze after she developed a fascination with the character of Dr. Frank N. Furter. The addition of physical performance was the final step in making *Rocky Horror* a true phenomenon. With all of the cult's practices in place, "audience participation finally had reached the level of true theatrics" (see Piro).

In order to say that the *Rocky Horror* experience is theatrical, it is important to understand how it can be defined in this manner. When we think of conventional theater, the image that comes to mind is a raised platform on which actors perform a written work composed by a playwright, with the audience seated in rows in front of the stage. Keeping respectfully quiet, the audience is only heard in relatively brief moments of reaction to the events on the stage and in the traditional round of applause upon the performers' completion of the performance. *The Rocky Horror Picture Show* in no way fits this conventional view. So how is it theatrical?

By Schechner's definition, a performance is not only the presentation of people on a stage, but "the whole constellation of events ... that take place in/among both performers and audience from the time the first spectator enters the field of the performance ... to the time the last spectator leaves" (1988:72), meaning that a performance is basically a collection of events between a performer and an audience. By traditional moviegoing standards, there is no question that *The Rocky Horror Picture Show* is a performance, because an audience enters the theater, views the film (performer), and leaves. These seemingly clear-cut lines get blurred, however, when the nature of the *Rocky Horror* environment is taken into account. Because so much of the experience comes from the audience's participation in the action, it becomes difficult to discern who really is the audience and who is the performer. For example, depending on when in the film they participate, it is entirely possible for an audience member to assume the role of both spectator and participant in the same performance. Even the tiniest interactions between audience and movie contain performance, as shown in the following example (note how the performer/spectator relationship shifts):

FRANK (AS PERFORMER): (film character sings) "Don't get strung out"/
AUDIENCE (AS SPECTATOR): silent.
AUDIENCE (AS PERFORMER): (interjecting live commentary) "on PCP"/
FRANK (AS SPECTATOR): silent.
FRANK (AS PERFORMER): "by the way I look"/AUDIENCE (AS SPECTATOR):
silent.
AUDIENCE (AS PERFORMER): "same thing"/FRANK (AS SPECTATOR): silent.
(Tal 1995)

Here, audience members interject commentary in the beats between
Frank's lines in a sort of conversation with the screen. In doing so, focus
is tossed back and forth as the audience serves as spectator for Frank to
perform his line while he, in turn, seems to pause for the audience's performance. Though the interplay is fast and furious, the elements of performance are always intact. The participants yell, they throw things, they
dress up, they lip-sync, they perform actions — there is no question that
this is theater, as Schechner defines it. Take the example above: while the
constant presence of performer and spectator creates a performance, the
actions (in this case, the lines "don't get strung out"/"on PCP") create theater. By the same token, the performance of the "Time Warp" and the
throwing of "cards for sorrow, cards for pain" during Frank's song, provide the set of actions taken during the "production" of the film, thus
endowing the film with the qualities of theater.

The Rocky Horror Picture Show also successfully holds true to Schechner's definition of "script." In the case of *Rocky Horror*, however, the script
is composed of both the filmic text as well as the audience utterances.
Everything that occurs at a *Rocky Horror* showing originated in the spec-
tator-performance script of the original regulars at the Waverly. They created and passed on every line, prop, and practice just by being there and
by being seen by others. When Louis Farese said, "Buy an umbrella, you
cheap bitch," it was heard by a theater full of people and thus passed on
as script. Subsequently, the people went on to repeat it at every showing
of the film, transmitting it each time to those who had never heard it. As
Rocky Horror fans branched out over the years to theaters across the country, Farese's phrase, together with the many others introduced at the
Waverly, was carried along, and hence transmitted to each new audience.
In the 1970s when the *Rocky Horror* "following" boomed at the Waverly,
there was no written record of any of the participation — it was only spread
through word of mouth. However, with the rise in popularity of the internet, fans have taken it upon themselves to create sites in which they have
published the film's libretto, word for word. Since the script has been written into an independent document, it can safely be defined as the "drama"

of the *Rocky Horror* experience. Furthering the transmittance of the drama, webpages can now be found that contain complete written documentation of the audience participation as well as the movie script.

In a site prepared and edited by Katzir Tal (*www.geocities.com/Hollywood/4198/script.txt*), fans come face-to-face with an introduction to every aspect of the film's performance, beginning with general information, including the prop list, imperative phrases that are universal to every *Rocky Horror* performance, the cast list, and various etiquette tips. Following the introduction and preparation is the complete libretto of the film, interjected with several options for audience response written in parentheses wherever applicable. Thus potential performers gain access to the knowledge of *Rocky Horror*'s theatrical action through the study of its drama. The performance of *Rocky Horror* does not stop at the theater, however.

In the late 1970s the Waverly regulars began to gather every weekend outside the theater, well before the start of the movie, to sing and dance and share in the camaraderie they found in being with other *Rocky Horror* devotees. The theater of the outside activities was later complemented by fan circulation of homemade newsletters—one later to become the official fan newsletter, *The Transylvanian*—and fan-generated quizzes allowing for the trading of *Rocky* trivia with other fans. These traditions have since survived the days at the Waverly, and continue still, over twenty years later, together with fan clubs, conventions, and any other performances that could be expected of a devoted cult. In addition, the myriad of different websites that have sprung up over the years include not only the movie and participation scripts like Tal's site, but also information pages, fan tribute sites extolling the film and/or favorite characters, and quiz game sites. Fans are not only participating in the live performances of *Rocky*, but they are creating performances of their own just by producing a webpage and having people view it.

The *Rocky Horror* cult is one of the largest and most popular of the twentieth century. But what exactly makes it a cult? Why has it endured for so many years, and why are fans so devoted to its camp? The answer lies not in the quality of the motion picture, but in a society that thrives on its need for the freedom of expression and the feeling of belonging. Culture may be a general way to define a country's people, but beneath that generalization lie countless different groups of varying views following different ways of life, and people who naturally organize themselves into functioning subcultures.

In his essay "Subculture Marginality," David Arnold defines "subculture" as "a set of conduct norms which cluster together in such a way that they can be differentiated from the broader culture of which they are a part" (1970:84). Also, he suggests that "since people live out their lives within subcultures, it is from participation in these subcultures (the interaction with other members) that they develop many if not all of their attitudes and patterns of behavior" (87). *Rocky Horror* followers function much in this way, in that they join together in performing the phenomenon, understanding one another's devotion, and celebrating what they love. Their actions and behavior when attending a *Rocky* showing set them apart from all other subcultures in society.

However, it is generally only during these showings that the subculture presents itself. *Rocky* fans do not usually go about their everyday lives immersed in the film and its traditions. They have ordinary lives, attending work or school and interacting with other people in society. Most devotees exist in other levels of society, in other subcultures in which they carry out their normal lives. On the weekends, they escape these lives to convene in the movie theater and exist in an alternate subculture — that which exists in *Rocky Horror*. A *Rocky Horror* subculture in everyday life would be illogical because singing, rice-throwing, and Transylvanian dancing do not fit well within ordinary existence. Also, in light of the fact that *Rocky Horror* is predominantly a performance subculture, it makes sense to say that it cannot exist constantly, just as an actor cannot spend every waking hour engulfed in a role.

Herein lies the appeal of the weekend *Rocky Horror* culture — "the attraction of subculture is its rebelliousness, its hedonism, its escape from the restrictions of work and home" (Brake 1985:191). The way the *Rocky Horror* subculture functions directly correlates to its existence as a cult. People are so devoted to this film, and have been for so many years, that they often live for the coming weekend when they can take part in the worship rituals of participation.

In his book *Collective Search for Identity* (1969), Orrin Klapp addresses the existence of cult devotion in society: "While such devotion cannot be called worship in the religious sense ... it is too serious to be dismissed as play, and is cultic in features such as centering, hero worship, and mystique not evident to the uninitiated. Any activity can be cultic at the point when a person not only does it but lives for it" (191). Though the behaviors and practices of the followers are intricate enough to qualify as a valid cultic subculture, they only exist with the movie. But such is the nature of the *Rocky Horror* cult — it exists in performance, and that performance can only exist when the film itself is involved.

The Rocky Horror Picture Show has affected our society in significant ways. True, it is a movie — a "cheesy," campy, SF/horror send-up, spoof, musical picture. In no way is it serious, nor is it meant to be taken seriously.

It is entertainment in its purest form, with no intention or necessity to have any kind of significant social impact, and perhaps the odd phenomenon it inspires will die out in coming years, to be remembered as a fad started by crazy kids in the 1970s. Yet the impact created by *Rocky Horror* has lasted for more than twenty years, creating an entire subculture among the droves of followers it has accumulated.

Perhaps it started because the earliest Waverly viewers felt they had to join in the shameless fun by poking fun back at the movie. Whatever the cause, the result has been turned into a major phenomenon that has given thousands of people a venue in which to express themselves. By appealing to our sense of humor, *Rocky Horror* allows for the performer in all of us to be revealed, setting us free from societal pressure and elitist snobbery. The more blatant, blunt, shocking, and fearless a participant, the better to show the cultic devotion to a silly, wonderful film. That devotion and personal expression brings people together in a way that most Oscar-winning motion pictures cannot, and that is what makes *The Rocky Horror Picture Show* an enduring cult classic.

The Rocky Horror Picture Show: *A No-Tech Virtual-Reality Film Experience*

BY MICHAEL URDANETA

The genesis of *Rocky Horror*'s American success was the night when the Waverly theater played the sound track before the film in order to warm up the audience, which responded in vaudevillian fashion, with boos and cheers. The audience had so much fun that regulars began to appear every weekend. One night, one of the regulars shouted out to the screen on which Janet was walking in the rain, "Buy an umbrella, you cheap bitch!" and "How strange was it?" in response to the criminologist/narrator's infamous "I would like, if I may, to take you on a strange journey." Eventually all of the regulars would shout out funny lines, interacting with the screen. Many were so amusing and fit so well that the rest of the audience picked them up. As fans moved from New York to other cities where the film was being shown, they brought the audience lines with them, spreading the more-or-less audience script that is followed like ritual today.

On Halloween, many of the regulars came in the costume of the characters in the film. This seemed to stick, and slowly more and more regulars wore increasingly intricate costumes to the show until they were nearly exact replicas of the onscreen performers. Another regular began dancing and lip-synching to the pre-show music and was immediately joined by others. When those in costume started getting into the act, it was only natural that they take on their respective roles in the lip-synch. This mimicry eventually bled into lines and actions from numbers during the film

135

and grew until the entire body of action and spoken word was mimicked throughout the theater by the "cast."

Schechner, in *Environmental Theater* (1994), described his 1960s experiences with The Performance Group in creating theater where the space between the performer and spectator blurred. The main points and ideas he lays out set environmental theater apart from conventional Western theater. In this kind of theater, "All the areas where the audience is and/or the performers perform ... are actively involved in all the aspects of the performance," Schechner explains (2). He then analyzes audience participation within the space of an environmental production:

> Participation occurred at those points where the play stopped being a play and became a social event — when spectators felt that they were free to enter the performance as equals. At these times the themes of the play — its "literary values" — were advanced not textually but wholly through action.... For spectators who participated, performers were no longer actors but people doing what they believed in, "spontaneously." It was impossible for most people to acknowledge that the attributes of "actor" and "person" were not mutually exclusive ... letting people into the play to do as the performers were doing, to "join the story" [44].

Toward the end of the book, Schechner includes a letter he wrote to an unnamed playwright whose work he was transforming into an environmental play: "We accept your words as written, and the parts that they are organized into, and the basic flow of the action ... we must work long and *hard to find our own places within the world of your script*. Or, to put it another way, we accept your script as *part of an artwork yet to be completed*" (236). With these observations and ideas in mind, perhaps *The Rocky Horror Picture Show* experience can be viewed as an environmental film.

"Restored behavior" plays a conspicuous part in the augmentation of this two-dimensional film. The "restored behavior" in *The Rocky Horror Picture Show* includes the costuming and reenactment of the film. The audience cast assumes various (if not all) "strips of behavior" from the performers in the film and "restores" them with slight alterations in the environment of the theatrical space. "Restored behavior is 'me behaving as if I am someone else' or 'as if I am beside myself, or not myself,' as when in trance" (Schechner 1985:37). The audience performers behave as if they are the characters onscreen, beside themselves, completing the same actions as the onscreen actors, but modified to fit the space of the theater. For example, during Rocky's first escape, the Frank N. Furter spectator chases the Rocky spectator around the audience — echoing the scene occurring onscreen in the laboratory. In order to bridge the gap between the imaginary world of the film ("out there") and the real world of the audience ("me"), the audience "restores" the action onscreen into the theater itself. It seems as if the characters, as in a child's fantasy tale, have stepped out of the screen (or the audience has stepped into the screen) and "gone through the looking glass." The characters are no longer separated from the audience by time and place (they are viewing events that took place in the past in another location, but the film has captured the images of the event). As a result, it is now perfectly possible to feel Dr. Frank N. Furter's biceps as he sings "I Can Make You a Man."

This does not stop with reenactment. Audience use of props is also a form of "restored behavior." Audience members who squirt water pistols restore the behavior of the environment within the film for the benefit of those whom the water "rains on." The audience cast replicates the film cast's performance, becoming the characters themselves. The audience members hit by water (or other props) become people within the diegetic world of the film: they are out in the rain, getting wet, desperate for the shelter of the castle. This reinforces the transportation of the audience to the original event (or vice versa) and further diminishes the distance caused by the two-dimensional property of the film.

The largest and most immediate contribution to the "environmental" effect is found in the audience lines. J. L. Austin would classify the recitation of the lines as a "performative utterance." He defines these performatives in two ways:

A. they do not "describe" or "report" or constate anything at all, are not "true or false"; and
B. the uttering of the sentence is, or is a part of, the doing of an action, which again would not normally be described as saying something. (1975:5)

While the lines are orchestrated and timed in such a way as to appear to have relevance to the film and the actions that take place in the film, they do not serve to truly describe, report, or judge the actions. In the Riff-Raff exchange the audience says, "Say hello, Riff-Raff" not to actually tell Riff-Raff to say "hello." To do so would do no good anyway, as film is not an interactive medium. The purpose is to give the *impression* that the audience is telling Riff-Raff to say "hello." The performative is set into a context in which it appears to be interactive. We see a similar substitution or disguise of a performative in Austin's example of marriage vows. To recite the vows is to enter the contract of marriage, but it is done with set lines that are not specifically descriptive to anything happening at that moment. (This is also a form of Schechner's "strips of behavior.")

Austin also states, however, that not only is a performative not descriptive nor a report, it is also the performance of an act. It may be difficult to look at an audience yelling lines at a screen as the performance of an act. Kurt Lancaster addresses a similar situation in his essay "The Longing for Prelapsarian Fantasies in Role-Playing Games." He describes performatives used in the course of role-playing: "The verbalization of a statement (such as, 'I do' at a wedding ceremony; or 'I,' as my character Devin Smith, 'draw my gun,' in a role playing game), comprises the action of what *is* done" (1998:51). He reasons that when one person gives a performative, it changes the context of the imaginary circumstances in everyone's head which make up the game: "The performative takes them out of a 'real world' frame into a 'fantasy world' frame of mind ... When the statement occurs, the players are *engrossed* within a fantasy, placed in the 'new context created by the [performative] utterance.'" (51; emphasis mine). When a *Rocky Horror Picture Show* fan utters an audience line, it engrosses or immerses the fan into the fantasy world of the film. This process is almost subconscious. As when Lancaster's role-players speak the performative and "do" the performative in their imaginary world, a *Rocky Horror Picture Show* fan speaks the performative and is at the same time entering into the diegetic world of the film and conversing with the characters within the film.

This phenomenon of augmentation/re-creation occurs with cherished objects in society. Roach explains, "Into the cavities created by loss through death or other forms of departures [people try to find] satisfactory alternatives" (1996:2). The film stays the same every night — there are no new twists, developments, or nuances, but the regulars want more. Their cherished film ends too soon, and there is no more material with the same cast and characters. However, a new piece of dialogue seamlessly inserted by an audience member during the course of the film can easily change the context of the entire conversation, thus creating an alternate (if not truly new) version of the film. For example (stage directions are in parentheses):

> RIFF-RAFF: Hello.
> BRAD: Hi! My name is Brad Majors, and this is my fiancé, Janet Weiss. I wonder if you could help us. You see our car broke down a few miles up the road. Do you have a phone we might use?
> RIFF-RAFF: You're wet.
> JANET: Yes— it's raining.
> BRAD: Yes.

RIFF-RAFF: Yes...
(Lightning strikes, illuminating motorcycles.)

The same scene with the audience lines (audience lines are in brackets):

RIFF-RAFF: Hello. ["and welcome to the crystal maze"]
["Brad, how do you feel?"]
BRAD: Hi! My name is Brad Majors, and this is my fiancé, Janet Weiss. I wonder if you could help us. You see our car broke down a few miles up the road. Do you have a phone we might use?
RIFF-RAFF: ["Look between Janet's legs."] You're wet.
["No shit, Sherlock"]
["Hey Janet, are you gay?"]
JANET: Yes ["Why?"] — it's raining. ["No shit"]
["Brad, are you gay?"]
BRAD: Yes.
["Riff, are you gay?"]
RIFF-RAFF: Yes...
["God, are you gay?"]...
(Lightning strikes, illuminating motorcycles.)
["Sorry. Just kidding"]
["You weren't supposed to see that!"]

(*www.cs.wvu.edu/~paulr/rhps/rhps.html*)

Restored behavior in the context of reenactment also serves as a form of Roach's surrogation. Seeing the film as an "environmental" theater, an audience member, already familiar with the film, may be drawn to other instances of the film presentation to see the live cast and the nuances and interpretations of the new actors. In one such example, the live Riff-Raff was much more evil and commanding than his filmic counterpart. During the "Toucha-Toucha-Toucha-Touch Me" number between Rocky and Janet, the live cast was much more sexually explicit, and, during close-ups or scenes in which neither character could be seen well, the live actors created their own blocking, including a standing sexual sixty-nine position. This type of improvisation and interpretation makes the story and the performance fresh. The film playing on the screen behind the actors keeps the integrity and flow of the film the same, however, so that it cannot corrupt the story or performance so much that it is unrecognizable or anything less than the celebrated genius of *Rocky Horror*. The environmental film medium allows for a very strict, and therefore always satisfying, surrogate of the film.

The Rocky Horror Picture Show has evolved with no real objective in mind other than having fun. Oddly enough, its development has employed the well-studied and subtly intricate performance devices of restored behavior and performatives. It has become a perfect counterpart of The Performance Group's environmental theater in the arena of film. This film has transformed into three dimensions and beyond without any flimsy technology. It is now a no-tech virtual-reality film experience. Anyone can step into the world of *Rocky Horror* because of the dedication and benign fanaticism this cult classic has produced.

PART VI

Marketing and Playing with Action Figures

Action Figures:
Props of Performance

BY VERA ZAGO

Walking around the crowded floor, I glanced at the various tables. There were several comic book dealers. After all, this was the "Big Apple Comic Book and Toy Show." There were also many tables full of my memories. I hesitated at one of these tables and picked up a worn-out Lion-O figure, remembering how my brother and I used to watch the animated series *Thundercats* every day after school. He had acquired several of the action figures through persuasion tactics that he performed on my parents during many trips to the mall or local store with a toy department. This Lion-O figure had other companions lying on the table beside him: Panthero, Cheetara, and Mummra. Each figure had the marks that could only be the result of repeated playings. The dealer looked up at me, but he was probably used to people looking at remnants of their childhood and so he continued reading his magazine.

As I began to cross the floor again, another table caught my eye. On the floor were various bins of action figures in plastic baggies, some still clinging onto their accessories, while others were bare. Digging through the bin, I found some old relics. I came across old *He-Man* figures. I didn't know that, back in 1982, these figures were the result of a clever marketing scheme from the union of a toy company, Mattel, and an animation company, Filmation, or that the figures would make a worldwide profit of $500 million. Some 125 million character dolls were sold in the United States alone, an average of eleven to every American boy between the ages of five and ten (Pecora 1998:69). Memories of battles that I staged with friends, as we combined our collection of *He-Man and the Masters of the*

Universe action figures, were recollected while I looked at the old action figure in my hand. Sometimes we could begin our play only after watching the half-hour animated cartoon, which always presented the same themes of the hero that overcomes evil with the aid of his companions. He-Man had a Superman-like transformation from a prince to the ultimate warrior, the rival of all that was bad, Skeletor. The show would inspire us to carry out the narrative themes with our little physical props: replicas of the characters we would view on television.

The concept of action figures may have started in 1920, when the editors of *Playthings* magazine suggested that toys should be made in the likeness of American heroes such as George Washington, Abraham Lincoln, and Theodore Roosevelt, as well as based upon such roles as the soldier, businessman, actor, hunter, and western settler. Eventually, space toys appeared shortly after the success of Sputnik in 1957 and Apollo in the 1960s. By the 1980s, toy companies developed many products that combined fantasy with skill, such as Simon, an active game in which children attempted to push lit panels (accompanied by a tone) in the same sequence that it presented the lights and tone to them. The toy's sounds and lights were similar to the spaceship seen at the end of *Close Encounters of the Third Kind*. However, another science-fiction film would launch a whole new line of toys and change the toy market forever: *Star Wars*. Kenner produced the figures, which were an average height of three and three-quarter inches, making them small enough to fit into a child's hand and also to fit into various vehicles and battleships. Children and fans of the film became excited that their science-fiction fantasy could cross into the physical with these small representations of the characters. The success of the action figures was phenomenal, and with the launch of a second series in the 1990s, together with the release of the remastered *Star Wars* trilogy, as well as *The Phantom Menace*, once again the toy market released more *Star Wars* toys.

Several other toy companies tried to duplicate the success of Kenner by making action figures of similar size and based on films or television shows. Mattel arrived at success with the invention of *He-Man and the Masters of the Universe* in 1982. Working with Filmation, they devised a plan in which children would watch a short animated television show, which would inspire them to go out and buy toys related to that show. Commercials for the action figures and playsets were featured during the breaks to waken the young audience to the consumer possibilities. As a result, the action figures literally flew off the shelves of many stores. Figures became more and more complex. For example, some were made that could squirt water out of their mouth or had a fuzzy covering to simulate moss for a character that was covered in the organic substance. Following the success of the *He-Man* line came other series such as *Teenage Mutant Ninja Turtles* and *Mighty Morphin Power Rangers*. All of these successful series involved science-fiction and fantasy themes.

Television and film provide many different levels of entertainment for the audiences of today, and science fiction is the one genre in these media that reaches a diverse group, including children and adults. The overall theme of the science-fiction film or the general dramatic television program, such as good versus evil, is not entirely new because it has existed for some time in the conventional narratives. However, the mixture of this theme with the fantastical and imaginative defines the genre and makes it stand out among other types of narrative and performance. This fantastical element combined with the traditional narrative makes science fiction all the more appealing to children. Since the process of producing such science-fiction programs and films is indeed a business, this appeal is extremely useful in the production of objects, reflecting the program or film, with which children will play. Ever since the overwhelming popularity of shows such as *Star Trek* and films such as *Star Wars*, toys have served an important role in the success of the science-fiction movie or television show. Children encounter an array of action figures and dolls with which they may reenact what they have watched in any particular show or movie. Children use their play tactics and the objects marketed to them by various toy companies to create a sort of personal performance piece. When children interact and play with science-fiction action figures, they perform such traditional roles of heroes versus villains prevalent in narratives, but broaden their play into the realm of fantasy. Further, in watching children play with such toys, one can recognize their play as a performance.

To understand why children play with action figures, it is necessary to examine the family structure, in which children are often placed in a position in which they are left out of most of the responsibilities. With the use of toys such as action figures, children can create their own world. They can feel responsible and in a position of control over what they make their action figures do. In addition, children can use their play as a constructive way to work out aggressions and feelings over personal events or occurrences in their daily lives. Child psychologist Erik Erikson writes that "the pleasure of mastering toy things becomes associated with the mastery of the traumas which were projected on them, and with the prestige gained through such mastery" (quoted in Konner 1991:176). Children play to feel that they have control over a world that they create. Erikson believes that when dealing with imaginary figures supplied by the media, peers, and parents, children prepare for a complex reality when mastering an even more complicated fantasy acted out with these action figures (Mergen 1986:132).

Brian Sutton-Smith, in *Toys as Culture*, contends that play takes on a new meaning rather than representing something that may or may not be physically real, but really the role of play is to express the desires of the player. Playing is a method of communication of the impossible and/or the wants of the person playing. For example, a child playing with a fire truck may be acting out his desire to become a firefighter. Another example could include a child who is playing with a Luke Skywalker action figure in a X-Wing fighter. The child may be acting out desires to battle the forces of evil in space or to become a Jedi Knight, even though it is realistically impossible. Noted child psychologist Jean Piaget proposes that "the child's mind is powerful enough to generate fantasies, but not mature enough to compare them to logic," adding that by age three, children are able to pretend using languages and symbols to make a world for themselves (quoted in Konner 1991:172). Children translate images and sounds from their mental imagination to the physical with skits and productions they perform with their action figures. Often a child puts on a performance with action figures to entice others to participate. For example, a child may play with a Lion-O figure from the *Thundercats* television show in order to get a reaction from a nearby child playing with Lion-O's archrival, Mummra. While playing together, each child presents his or her character and waits for the reaction and response of the other. This adheres to Goffman's definition of a performance: "an activity of a given participant on a given occasion which serves to influence in any way any of the other participants" (1959:15).

Schechner proposes that the "self can act in a set of roles" (1985:36). The roles that a child performs while playing with action figures can serve as an example. One playing with an action figure such as He-Man can perform the roles of that character he or she has watched on the show. For example, the child may reenact the transformation the prince endures to become He-Man or a preparation for battle with Skeletor. In either case, the child is performing the actions that He-Man would take as part of the narrative of the television show. The child learns all of the actions through repeated viewings of the show and adapts them to his or her own behavior in play methods. This leads to Schechner's second point, that performance is never for the first time but is rather "twice-behaved behavior" (36). A child can never present the animated performance of his or her favorite *He-Man* episode or for the stories in the *Star Wars* trilogy; however, the child can use the props offered by peers, parents, and the media (namely action figures) to rehearse what he or she has watched. These rehearsals become the building blocks in constructing the overall narrative or feel of the show the child has viewed. "During rehearsals," Schechner posits, "a past is assembled out of bits of actual experience, fantasies, historical research, and past performance" (52). For example, a child can play with Han Solo and Jabba the Hut in one instance, and, in the next, play with Luke Skywalker. Both events differ in the use of characters, but combine to reenact the various plotlines of the *Star Wars* trilogy. The overall motive is to refer back to the source of inspiration and excitement. The feeling of the fantastical and exciting is one which the child finds favorable, so he or she tries to reenact this with action figure props. Again, with these specific, specialized toys, children come closer to re-creating the magic and fantasy they experienced while watching the program.

It is almost impossible to find a children's film or television show that is without a line of action figures or playthings. Television production and film companies understand the importance of toys for the overall success of their project. As a result, action figures are produced in mass quantities and advertised frequently to entice young viewers. Young viewers, bombarded with commercials (combined with a favorable and fantastical experience they may have with the show), are influenced to purchase these products. Once they take these toys home and take them out of the packaging, the possibilities to reconstruct the wonder and adventure shown to them on their favorite television shows and films are endless and add to the child's development. And as some of them grow into adults, they may become "collectors"— adults who collect action figures as a way to relive their childhood.

Action Figures: Another Style of Performance

BY HEATHER JEWELS

Action figures provide fans with a kind of performance that is different from acting in a conventional play or film, engaging in a role-playing game, or any other means of assuming a role in one's favorite fantasy experience. Unlike these other forms, with action figures the drama stems from the figurines themselves and from the needs of the performers involved.

A typical action figure comes packaged neatly in a bubble pack. Often, the packaging re-creates the atmosphere of the original television show or film in which the character usually dwells. These packages also carry some background information concerning the character, lists of accessories, and a brief story. *Star Trek* and *Babylon 5* action figures, for example, are especially faithful to this formula, as were the old *Teenage Mutant Ninja Turtles* figures.

Some performers (or "collectors," as they are also called) prefer to keep their figures in the packaging, to keep them safe and free from performance "injury." One such person uses his *Star Wars* figures, in their full packaging, as wallpaper in his room. However, the typical performer chooses to break out the figure from its protective packaging and use the accessories to assist in this unique form of performance.

Performances of this sort can vary greatly, depending on such circumstances as figure availability and the general mood of the performer. Schechner notes that "moods are especially liable and can shift suddenly and totally. A serious injury can change the tone of a football game ... but once the wounded are carried from the field, the mood changes back to the playful" (1993:26). I found this to be particularly true when holding action figure games with one group of friends. Using a variety of *Star Trek* figures, we would improvise scenarios that involved crossovers and life-threatening alien forces. Depending on our moods, we would create sinister villains such as Evil Looseleaf Man and Scary Severing Scissors, or happy scenarios that would see our heroes safely through the day. One performance featured myself and friends Kathleen and Laura (hereafter referred to by initial):

> H: HAHHAAAAAAA! I AM SCARY SEVERING SCISSORS! I HAVE COME TO CHOP YOU TO PIECES, LIEUTENANT BARCLAY!
>
> K: Oh, um, oh no! Please, please, could you spare my life? I mean, I've barely proven myself worthy of working on the *Enterprise*! P-please, don't sever my limbs!
>
> H: TOO LATE, WORTHLESS HUMAN! I WILL HAVE TO SEVER EVERY PART OF YOU IN AN EFFORT TO CLEANSE HUMANITY OF ITS WORTHLESSNESS!
>
> L: Ha ha! But I am Commander Will Riker, and with my manliness, I will save you, Barclay!
>
> (Riker figure battles with scissors, eventually knocking them over onto their side.)
>
> K: Oh, oh, thank you, Commander! I owe you my life! I'll do anything for you!
>
> H: CURSES, FOILED AGAIN! I SHALL RETURN! HAHHAHAHHAHA HAHAHA!

Often these sort of performances— which spring, perhaps, from more ill-tempered moods— served to cheer up the participants.

Another way in which action figures are a source of performance is by allowing the players to control their own stories. Often they can use the figures to physically act out things they would not be able to see, hear, or control themselves, because the performance of a television show or film is primarily non-interactive. For example, I was always a big fan of the Kira-Odo relationship on *Star Trek: Deep Space Nine*, and as soon as I had obtained my Kira and Odo action figures, I promptly made sure they were always displayed somewhere — always in some sort of affectionate pose. One of my teachers later commented that she missed my "little dolls" once I had stopped carrying them around.

Before I had the action figures, I had to create my own. For example, I would often carry around bookmarks of them and show them to friends. I also fondly recall making paper dolls of my favorite characters that had not been made into action figures. The public television show *Square One TV* had its own series-within-a-series, entitled *Mathnet*. The Mathnetters were doomed never to be released as action figures. So I drew my own paper versions, to be used to star in their own adventures over which I had ultimate control.

Another aspect that enhances the action figure experience is that performers get to choose which of the characters they become. The action figure market has become larger as time has progressed, and demand has grown. Playmates Toys' *Star Trek* series has grown from a few *Next Generation* figures to an entire line of products, including fly-them-yourself *Enterprises*, "working" tricorders, and even pocket-sized replicas of the Borg ship (rivaling the little girls' "Polly Pocket" series) in which one can "assimilate" from the palm of one's hand.

Tomart's Action Figure Toy and Review Magazine gives prices, tips, styles, and hot news about the newest action figures. In one old issue I have, the special news pages "dish" collectors on which figures are likely to become rare and how much one should expect to pay for such figures. The center of the magazine is filled with large guides to pricing the figures. Certain figures have different variations that make the playing capacity vary, and their value more: *Teenage Mutant Ninja Turtles*, for example, lists several different April O'Neill figures. The prices vary based on production year, number, and popularity. The original April figures, for example, are much rarer and more sought after than the newer ones, and are therefore more expensive. Potential performers are willing to spend this money in order to enhance their playing options.

Webpages house online ordering and also provide the latest up-to-the-minute news. There are several devoted to Playmates' *Star Trek* series, offering pictures, prices, and even online purchasing options. These websites assist prospective performers (or the seasoned veterans) in expanding their casts of figurines. One site allows the ultimate "choose your own adventure": vote on which action figures should be produced. Anyone who always wanted to act out that scene between *Star Trek*'s Kirk and one of his women can now choose their favorite one and vote (*www.unc.edu/~lbrooks2/playmate.html*). Other webpages also allow for webmaster performers to display their ideas and handiwork for all to see — an online performance. One such page, entitled "Action Figures, the Musical!" provides a nice little crossover of *Star Wars*, *Bye Bye Birdie*, and *Les Misérables*. As it says (humorously) on the page:

> Now you too can have a poseable action figure from *Les Misérables*, The Musical Sensation! Recreate your favorite scenes from this moving tale of love and death in nineteenth-century France. You can pretend that you are locking up Jean Valjean unjustly, or that you are shooting young Gavroche in the prime of his life. You can even steal the accessories from the dead bod-

ies. Change the plot of Victor Hugo's epic novel! Make Young Cosette commit suicide, or have Javert wed Marius! (*www.cc.gatech.edu/gvu/people/ Phd/Noel.Rappin/GravityWeb/actionfiguresthemusical.html*)

Additionally, other sites provide pricing information, pictures of toys, and other such helpful hints as where to find them, and when.

Finally, action figures differ from any other sort of performance because the performers are involved with an object that feeds their instincts. A role-playing game, for example, may be composed of certain pre-scripted behavior, the success of actions, perhaps, determined by the roll of dice. Since one is controlling the action figure, it becomes more of an extension of oneself, and can also become more physically active with another action figure, with no fear of serious injury other than the occasional chip (of course, there are always the random decapitations). On the other hand, it could be said that action figures are a lesser form of performance because they are providing a character instead of creating one. Nevertheless, they are in their own class of performance as a popular, treasured, and often-enjoyed activity. They provide an escape that is different from role-playing games and other forms of performance since they offer many variations.

Whatever the reason, one thing is clear: action figures are here to stay as objects of performance for a long time to come. If you don't believe me, just go to your local toy store and see for yourself. Who knows, you just might come out with your own special performance figures!

The Action of Star Wars Comes Home

BY DAVID RODRIGUEZ

Some of the most beautiful sights in New York City surround you as you come to F. A. O. Schwarz at the northeast corner of Fifth Avenue and 58th Street. Pictures of the talking plush toy "Furby" cover the windows, hovering over a line of people outside just waiting for these lovable stuffed creatures. Despite the long line wrapped around the building, you push toward your destiny inside.

After revolving through the doors, you are immersed into toy heaven. Stuffed animals fill your every sight. A toy song plays from a spinning clock welcoming you to your paradise of child's play. There is no sign of your destination in front of you, and you realize that you must open your Jedi senses to the power of the Force as Obi-Wan had to when looking for the shut-off switch to the tractor beam in *Star Wars: A New Hope*.

Suddenly you are swept into a sea of tourists and New Yorkers, from young to old, dressed in casual jeans and T-shirts to formal attire. You swim through the crowds passing Blues Clues, a giant bear, and Grizzly Falls on your right and Adoption Spot on your left. A huge robot towers over you. You hear the robot repeatedly say that he will take you upstairs to the second level. But you resist this trap by the dark side of the Force and struggle on as Luke struggled through the frozen tundra of Hoth after escaping the Wampa cave in *The Empire Strikes Back*.

Stairs come up to you suddenly, and you see a glimpse of salvation at the other end despite Balzac balls of every imaginable size bouncing in front of you. Moving on, you see a taxi and Lady Liberty high above you with one last reminder that you really are in New York City. The Empire even goes so far as to play a Jedi mind trick on you by playing the song "New York, New York." However, they make one fatal mistake with this trap: it is someone besides Franky singing it.

This insight gives you the power for which you have been waiting. You rush forward with the choir music from when Luke was defeating his father in *Return of the Jedi* playing in your mind. Then you hear it. It crawls inside you and you begin to feel the Force all around you. The familiar theme music from the opening title sequences transforms you into the powerful Jedi that you are destined to be. You have entered the *Star Wars* toy section at F. A. O. Schwarz!

The people in the store have all been taken to another world. Yes, they are still in F. A. O. Schwarz in New York City, but in this toy section they are in the world of *Star Wars*. The toys represent the world that many have watched and wished they were a part of. Many people have dreamed of being Luke Skywalker, Han Solo, or Princess Leia. The toys allow fans to do that. They take a person into a world in which he or she desires to be. A fantasy world is re-created every time that person plays with the toys. It could be said, in Schechner's nomenclature, that a person "restores behavior" by playing with the toys (1985:35), the behavior being restored built on the characters that were performed by the actors in the original movies. Action figures are a direct reconstruction of characters in the *Star Wars* movies. When a person plays with these figures, he or she restores "strips of behavior" seen in the films. The actions of the characters can be restored any way the person wants to play with them. When people play, they are putting themselves into a fantasy world. Play is a way to release oneself from everyday life. Also, it "is a structuring activity, the activity out of which understanding comes. Play is at one and the same time, the location where we question our structures of understanding and the location where we develop them" (Hans 1981:x). In playing, we begin to understand ourselves. The action figures, then, afford the opportunity to discover our dreams and desires, allowing us to imagine what it would be like to fight Imperial storm troopers, or even to be so evil as to destroy an entire planet. Restoring the behavior of *Star Wars* action figures through play allows one to live in a fantasy universe for a time.

An Australian gentleman at F. A. O. Schwarz notes why there is such an appeal to *Star Wars* toys: "It's the world that George Lucas created. We all want a part of that world for us. And just for the fun of it. Plus, there is the collector's aspect of it. But, you know, it's fun." The toys provide a connection to the movies. They are a link to the *Star Wars* universe that can be called upon anytime a person desires. Anytime the world is too crazy, one can reenter a fantasy universe where one makes the rules. A worker at F. A. O. Schwarz explains that the reason why so many people come to the *Star Wars* section at the store is "the movies. It's *Star Wars*. There's such a range of toys. It's not just the figures. One character has so many toys [representing her or him]. [Laughs.] It's *Star Wars*." This feeling seemed to be expressed by a majority of the people at the store. Some described how they used to play with the toys when they were younger, or how they wanted their kids to play with them. To some, it was nostalgic to see toys with which they had played for the first time fifteen, twenty years ago. As a result, the feelings felt in the films are experienced all over again as the world of *Star Wars* is all around them.

For some people, this phenomenon of keeping *Star Wars* memorabilia with them all of the time has transformed into hobbies and lifestyles. For these people, the ability to be part of the *Star Wars* universe goes far beyond one play session with action figures— it becomes an intricate part of their daily lives. At F. A. O. Schwarz, "collector toys" fill an entire section, and their packages clearly state that they are "For adult collectors only. This is not a toy." One can purchase a replica of the Darth Vader costume or Han Solo in the frozen carbonite. These toys allow adults to journey into the *Star Wars* universe in a different way than just playing with the action figures. The cover of the seventy-second edition of the *Action Figure News and Toy Review* features a picture of the Anakin Skywalker twelve-inch doll, the new item in the *Star Wars Masterpiece Edition*. The main article describes the content of the Masterpiece Edition, the twelve-inch doll, and reviews a book entitled *Anakin Skywalker: The Story of Darth Vader*. The last paragraph of the article states that "the appeal of Darth Vader to millions of fans around the world is astounding. The labored, mechanical breathing, the blood-red lightsaber, and the foreboding mask have inspired fear and fascination in audiences for two decades now" (Lee 1988:7). The seriousness of *Star Wars* toys is exemplified in this article, with one toy given a two-page write-up in the magazine. Collectors have become so involved in the *Star Wars* universe that the value of an original figure is unimaginable. According to the price guide in the back of the *Action Figure News and Toy Review* #72, the Jawa figure from its first release in 1978, with a plastic cape and still in its original packaging, is worth approximately $3,000. Thus, since *Star Wars* means everything to these collectors, they are willing to spend a lot of money to be close to the *Star Wars* experience. It may not be an exaggeration to say that being a part of this pop culture has transformed lives.

The *Star Wars Galaxy Collector* is a magazine especially devoted to the *Star Wars* collector. This official Lucasfilm magazine gives readers inside scoops on the *Star Wars* universe. In the third issue, the editor, Bob

Woods, explains why it is so much fun to be a fan: "[It] is the fantasy and inventiveness that the timeless tale affords. Starting from the canon, one can concoct his or her own addenda, creating characters, or weapons, or aliens, or starships, or battles that fit into one's private universe" (1998:2). This quote is linked with an article in the magazine explaining how easy it is to customize your own action figure. The article takes the reader through a step-by-step example in creating an action figure for Biggs Darklighter, Luke's friend from Tatooine. This new composite action figure is constructed by taking the body and jacket of Luke in ceremonial outfit, the head of Lando Calrissian in skiff-guard disguise, and the cape of Garindan, all to customize their own Biggs figure. Thus customizers have taken the action figures to a new level, one in which they are so in control of their *Star Wars* universe that they can create figures that are not even in production.

In the same issue, an article by Steve Sansweet describes his personal journey into the *Star Wars* universe. He began buying the toys when the movies came out, but he would only play with them a little bit. Then he would put them in a box and bury them under his neighbor's house. Eventually, with the neighbor's impending move, Steve dug them up and discovered that he had sixty-three bagged cartons of toys. He looked inside them to see which ones he owned, and then he started to buy the ones he still needed to complete his collection. Over the years he kept on collecting, to the point where the entire lower level of his house was taken over by the *Star Wars* universe. Sansweet became a "regular" at conventions, buying everything he could get his hands on. Eventually, in 1996, he quit his regular job of more than twenty years to become a roving convention ambassador to Lucasfilm, writing the *Star Wars Encyclopedia*. In a way, he has totally immersed himself into the *Star Wars* universe. Some fans try to "restore behavior" for a moment in time, but Sansweet has restored the entire *Star Wars* universe into his everyday life. According to Sansweet, if the fantasy of being a part of that universe ever dissipates, he can no longer function in life in the same way.

Toys give people something tangible with which to escape because people can create and manipulate them to suit their own purposes. Miniature worlds are created right before their eyes, and they become the masters of those worlds. No rules are made and restrictions on what can be done exist, except through the limits of the players' own imaginations. Action figures are toys frozen in time. The figure is forever in one gesture and in one costume, but it is never really the same in any situation because the player can create new scenarios. The specific behaviors established in the movies can be restored in the action of the toys, and a performance is created allowing the performer to be active as both player and spectator. The performer, by "playing," is brought into the universe of *Star Wars*, which can be so desirable as to consume its admirer's life completely. One only has to dream of being side by side with Luke Skywalker, Han Solo, Chewbacca, Princess Leia, C-3PO, and R2-D2 to understand the power of action figure performance.

When the time comes to leave the *Star Wars* universe at F. A. O. Schwarz, you take one last look at the universe that you so desire to be a part of and then make your way back to the front door. You pass the taxi and Lady Liberty, up the stairs, and past the evil-talking elevator robot, Blues Clues, Grizzly Falls, the spinning clock, and the long line of people still waiting anxiously for the Furby dolls. The doors revolve one more time, and you are confronted with hundreds of New Yorkers, car horns, cabs, and carriages. Suddenly, a voice calls out to you, "Remember, the Force will be with you. Always." You smile and realize that your destiny in the real universe awaits you.

PART VII

Performing in Role-Playing Games

The Performance of William Gibson's Tropes *in* Cyberpunk 2020

BY J. T. DORR-BREMME

> *"You saw them on me?"*
> *Thompson's eyes are cold, slate-like. You could write anything you wanted in them.* "Get real," *he grates,* "These were pros. If I'd jumped in, we'd both be dead." *The eyes appraise him.* "You've been off the Street too long, Rocker. You think everyone has a nice agent, a couple Solos covering their butts, and a comfy apartment like this somewhere. I let you take it, because I knew it would take at least five minutes for you to bleed yourself dry. I waited for them to move on, then used my Trauma Card." *There is a longish silence. Then,* "Look, Rocker. You want to guilt-loop, or you want to get your girl back?"
> *"So name names," says Johnny. He sits down on the edge of the bed, favoring his stapled side. He reaches for the tequila and takes a slug.*
>
> — From "Never Fade Away" in
> R. Talsorian Games's role-playing game
> *Cyberpunk 2020*

The "cyberpunk" subgenre is a recent creation in the science-fiction community that melds high technology with a collapsed society. William Gibson, with the publication of *Neuromancer* in 1984, has been widely acknowledged as one of the originators of this genre, and his novels have provided the framework for the role-playing game (RPG) *Cyberpunk 2020* (1990). This game has taken Gibson's ideas and created a detailed, near-future world in which class divisions are large, everyday life is dangerous,

159

and high technology is ubiquitous. Now, with more and more of Gibson's visions coming closer to reality, the game holds a special place in the greater realm of role-playing games; it is one of the few RPGs set in a world that could become a reality in the players' lifetimes. This essay will explore how tropes from both Gibson's novels and from today's high-technology society are absorbed into this game performed by the players.

Essentially, an RPG is an interactive oral fiction. That is to say, a group of people come together to improvise a complete story, affecting its outcome as they go. One member of this group, the gamemaster, devises a skeleton of a story, knowing its major plot points and supporting characters. Each other member of the group (a "player") has created a character to perform in the gamemaster's story; this is the "role-playing" aspect of the game. Each player uses the rule book to assemble a character sheet containing the characters' attributes, skills, personal appearance, profession, and possessions. This sheet is the players' interface immersing them into the game. It allows them to be and do things that the player may not be or do in ordinary life. There are no words, no pictures, and no game board for an RPG. The playing field is composed of the imaginations of the performers and the rules of the game. And each of these players envisions his or her character in the situation provided by the gamemaster and proceeds to perform the character, hoping to achieve whatever goal is set before them by the gamemaster's plot. Theatrical elements are visible in role-playing games. Similar to the art of acting, an RPG presents an imaginary situation to a player who must perform an assumed personality to achieve a certain goal in the game. The players, through *Cyberpunk 2020*, continue the entertainment provided by Gibson's works.

As the fantasy world keeps changing, so does the player's personal stake in it. Part of this change comes from William Gibson's own effect on society. He invented a near-future world that we seem to be approaching today, in which technology is such an integral part of our daily lives that it becomes grafted onto our bodies as implants or limb replacements. Gibson uses the term *cyberspace* in his novels to describe the graphic representation of earth's data. While perhaps these things seemed farfetched in 1984, the date of Gibson's first influential novel, *Neuromancer*, many of these formerly fictional ideas are being researched or created now. With the formerly disparate realms of reality and science fiction approaching each other, the fan's desire for cyberpunk increases. Indeed, even in the general public, the interest in high technology has grown as a status symbol and personal convenience (if not a necessity).

The attraction of the cyberpunk genre, however, is that of the familiar made strange. With technology as widespread as it is today, there is a

large amount of material in the *Cyberpunk 2020* game book that is familiar to a modern urbanite, but taken to the next step in technological or
societal evolution. For instance, virtually everyone in both the novels and
the RPG has a cellular phone/modem, a laptop computer, and a gun. This
portable technology is nothing new, nor is the increasing presence of
weapons. Gibson has taken today's technology and expanded it to society
as a whole. The designers of *Cyberpunk 2020* intentionally make use of this
familiarity while placing their game in an imaginary society. Many elements of today's popular culture are intermingled in the game design as
well as in the cyberpunk genre as a whole. Thus, since the imaginary environment is founded primarily in daily reality, it is easily absorbed by the
players/readers. The very closeness of this material to the players' own
lives draws them into performing a future version of themselves in the
form of an RPG.

The game designers, whether conscious of it or not, have taken common bits of this material and used them as codes implanted within the
rules of the game. As theorized by Barthes, literary or cultural codes are
preexisting bits of knowledge that are taken to be universal and are used,
sometimes subconsciously, to manipulate an effect on the receiver. Among
the codes Barthes defines in his essay are metalinguistic, social, and narrative codes (1985:88). Game designers use codes in a similar way in game
books as a way to immerse the player/reader more deeply in the fictional
environment of the game. Essentially, codes are effective ways of manipulating the players' thoughts or feelings in a particular direction through
the use of a subconscious understanding.

Besides the estranged familiarity of the cyberpunk environment that
intrigues the role-players, there is clearly a fan base for Gibson's work that
is fascinated with the possibility of immersion in Daniel Mackay's imaginary entertainment environment (2001:29). We have seen how these fans
wish for more consistent entertainment in this genre, and so the players
of *Cyberpunk 2020* desire to delve deeper into the still-unfinished world
that Gibson has created, indulging in what is known as "surrogation."
William Gibson still writes novels, but he is not a prolific author, and there
is typically a gap of several years between releases. With this dearth of an
ongoing cyberpunk entertainment, Gibson's fans can find and create new
stories in *Cyberpunk 2020*. This allows them to become personally involved
in the genre. Joseph Roach calls this process surrogation. The need for
surrogation is not a need for replacement per se, but rather a desire for
prolongation of one kind of performance that has ended prematurely.
For cyberpunk fans, this is the case with Gibson's novels. In carrying out
this process of surrogation, the role-players perform characters whose

professions and lifestyles are generalizations of the source characters in the novels.

Surrogation, as defined by Roach, is a process that "does not begin or end but continues as actual or perceived vacancies occur.... Into the cavities created by loss through death or other forms of departure, I hypothesize, survivors attempt to fit satisfactory alternates" (1996:2). In the introduction to his book, Roach gives an example of this theory when applied to the retirement of a professor and the way that his departmental colleagues both remember his work and work harder themselves in his absence. But in a way, surrogation applies to the world of cyberpunk as well. There is a "perceived vacancy" of cyberpunk entertainment (not enough Gibson novels), and through the creation of their characters, players of the *Cyberpunk 2020* remember the works of Gibson that created their imaginary playing field. Then, through their performance in gaming sessions, the players and the gamemaster demonstrate that the body of cyberpunk work is ever-growing. They themselves are adding to it with their performances, which they have in turn drawn from the preexisting body of Gibson's work.

Cyberpunk 2020 takes Schechner's "strips of behavior" from cyberpunk novels, with the game designers expanding on certain themes and adding certain elements of their own. With the repetition of these strips of behavior in the game, the players find themselves in a familiar yet fantastic world, performing characters in familiar yet original ways. With the very creation of this game, designers both honor and depart from their Gibsonian source. The players then immerse themselves in this imaginary environment and reconstruct more behaviors from the cyberpunk genre as a whole, and especially from Gibson. These repeated strips of behavior constitute a unique form of performance, according to Schechner's definition. With the *Cyberpunk 2020* game book and a few player-performers, the strips of behavior from Gibson's novels fulfill the players' need for a Gibson-novel surrogate.

These strips of behavior and tropes from the novels of William Gibson and society at large are performed in several different ways in the *Cyberpunk 2020* game. First of all, the game book contains several fine examples of tropes in the role-playing world that come from Gibson's source material for that world. The presence of these tropes in a form that is clear to a fan serves to make the game more accessible and immersive. In regard to immersion, the first chapter of the game book is an introduction to how the cyberpunk environment feels, and on the second page of the game book there is a list of concepts that are the "essence of the 2000s." One such concept is "Style Over Substance," or "It doesn't matter how well you do something, as long as you look good doing it" (1989:4). This directly mirrors many situations in Gibson's novels, especially in the following passage from *Mona Lisa Overdrive* regarding a fashion reporter whose personal fashion was observed: "Her only obvious augments were a pair of pale blue Zeiss [eye] implants. A young French fashion reporter had once referred to these as 'modishly outdated'; the reporter, Net legend said, had never worked again" (1988:185). It turns out that the woman with the implants was extremely bad at her job, but she did it with the correct flair to have influence. Clearly, a recognizable trope is being repeated in the game book, and in such a way, fans would recognize it and feel its familiarity. Therefore it is distilled by the game designers and made concrete, to be used as a reference point for creating the imaginary environment in the game.

Another example of Gibson's tropes being repeated and refined is in the creation of a character. In *Cyberpunk 2020*, players create their characters to have certain professions and attributes, much like any other RPG, but what makes *Cyberpunk* unique is its Lifepath. This is a flowchart of various events in each character's background, most of which is chosen by a random die roll, thereby making each character unique (although the chart is static). The Lifepath chapter distinctly reflects the dark, cyberpunk style of Gibson's characters. Through the rules, players are given many opportunities to create characters with dead or absent parents, an addiction, an enemy, or a failed romance. Certainly there are options for success, but the majority of cyberpunk is dark in this fashion. This does not directly reflect a single event or character in Gibson's works, but rather the overall tone of this genre. Most of Gibson's characters are people whom one would consider "seedy" if one met them on the street, and the game book takes this into account. For example, the characters in *Mona Lisa Overdrive* are a sixteen-year-old drug-addicted prostitute, the daughter of a Japanese gang boss, a Crime Lord who deals only in information, a killer for hire, and a group of squatters who have taken over a factory built on toxic landfill in order to build their robots and explore the Net.

These types of characters are also a repeated trope in the game, allowing players to perform some of the more exciting "professions" of the cyberpunk world. They are not all based on true professions, but in the imaginary entertainment environment of the game they are certainly valid character types who make a living in any number of ways. Using the examples above, one can place most of them into one of the roles, in the game's terminology, that a player could choose. For example, in *Cyberpunk 2020*'s terms, the killer for hire is a Solo, the squatters are Techies and Netrunners, and the Crime Lord is a Fixer. Each of these character types in the game is a distillation of what Gibson made available through his original writing. Some of the characters of *Mona Lisa Overdrive* are also found in two other seemingly unconnected novels, giving them a deeper background and making them feel more understood by the reader. This reiteration of characters is used in the game book as well, with various unique characters commenting, in side bars and text boxes, upon the rules. Each character is given a name and attitude, thereby helping the reader/player have a deeper understanding of the rules and how to deal with them in their imaginary, role-playing life.

In addition to containing many of these tropes, the game book also makes use of several codes from today's society in order to bring the reader/player closer to the material and make the environment more immersive. Mentioned previously were the metalinguistic, social, and narrative codes. Barthes defines the metalinguistic code as occurring when "one speaks of what one is going to say, if one doubles the language into two layers" (1985:88). This metalinguistic code is used by the game designers in the form of the recurring characters' commentary. By using these characters, they have not only introduced the rules but given the rules a reality. For example, there are four levels of wounds that a character can have: Light, Serious, Critical, and Mortal. In a sidebar next to the descriptions of these wound categories is the following: "You got a slice in the belly — that's a Light Wound. You got a ten-inch wedge taken out — that's a Serious Wound... — Ripperjack" (1989:117). Clearly, people in real life do not categorize their wounds in such a way. Yet through Ripperjack's explanation, the wound categories are defined in terms the players can visualize, because they are similar in tone to Gibson's novels.

The narrative code is used in conjunction with the metalinguistic code to make the reader/players desire an immersion into the performance experience of the game. According to Barthes, the "metalinguistic announcement has an aperitive function: it is a matter of whetting the reader's appetite. ... This 'appetizer' is a term of the narrative code" (1985:88). Thus, characters like Ripperjack have a dual function: to allow the designers to demonstrate their rules in the imaginary environment, and to allow the reader/players to imagine themselves performing their own characters within these rules. Another obvious use of a narrative code to draw in the audience is in the short story "Never Fade Away," quoted at the beginning of this essay. It introduces the reader to several characters living in the *Cyberpunk 2020* environment, and it unfolds a plot very similar, perhaps, to one in which the reader performs in the game. In addition to this, the characters and events described in the story are depicted as game statistics, making the story available as a playable adventure. By offering both a cyberpunk story and an introductory adventure, "Never Fade Away" is a well-designed "appetizer" for whetting the appetite of the reader/player.

Finally, Barthes's ideas of social codes are widely applied to make the *Cyberpunk 2020* world more reminiscent of Gibson's world, with which the reader/players are presumably familiar. The character types available to players are one good example of this. Barthes says that the social code allows the hero to be "socialized, made part of a defined society, in which he is provided with a civil title" (1985:88). In the *Cyberpunk 2020* game book, each character is provided with a title as well as a social standing. A clear example is found in the character description of a Fixer: "As a small time punk, you knew you had a knack for figuring out what other people wanted, and how to get it for them. For a price, of course. Now your deals have moved past the nickel-and-dime stuff into the big time ... You buy and sell favors like an old-style Mafia godfather" (1989:20). This generic Fixer is someone with a history and a goal, given a role to play in the crime-ridden cyberpunk world. In addition to giving "heroes" a place in the cyberpunk society, the game book has lengthy sections on drugs, Netrunning (a term for a cyberpunk hacker), and cybernetic implants, all of which can be found profusely in Gibson's novels. By describing in depth the way these elements can be used in the game, they are effectively "socialized" as well, given a place in the society in which the players will perform.

Clearly, the *Cyberpunk 2020* game book itself contains multiple re-performances of Gibson's tropes to create a familiar and immersive imaginary entertainment environment. These performances are then taken by the readers and players and themselves re-performed to create unique cyberpunk stories and characters. This process fulfills the players' desire for surrogation, helping to fill the gap between enjoyment of Gibson's novels and genuine personal involvement in that imaginary world. Within *Cyberpunk 2020* is the world of Gibson and more, making available to the players a completion of what the author had begun and allowing them to expand upon it to create their own stories and performances.

Ultima Online: *A Performance, or an Evolution Toward a Second Society?*

BY GEOFFREY AREND

> *It's more than a fantasy because it really exists,*
> *It's more than a game because it never ends,*
> *Go beyond life as you know it to an adventure*
> *More fantastic than you can imagine.*
> *Are you with us?*
> — opening mantra to the *Ultima Online* webpage

Ultima Online is the first of a new breed of role-playing games (RPGs), one that involves the internet. The player purchases the game, which contains a map and CD-ROM containing the program. Once the software is loaded, the player has to purchase a monthly subscription (billed to a credit card) to access the company's main database — the site where players from all over the world virtually meet each other as their characters online. Traditionally, an RPG involves a gamemaster (a person who controls the narrative of the adventure) and a group of players who assume different characters in the established "world." What Origin Systems has done with *Ultima Online* is to make the gamemaster a computer entity, thus allowing it to keep track of thousands of players at once, while keeping several subplots in the overall narrative constant. Though this is an achievement unto itself, what is truly remarkable is how Origin Systems has gone about promoting *Ultima Online* and how the players have taken it and propelled its evolution past a performance of a genre of fantasy to that of a performance of our society. Before beginning a discussion of *Ultima Online*, one should have an idea of what an RPG is and where its roots are as a cultural form.

Gary Gygax and Dave Arneson, under the company name of Tactical Studies Rules (TSR) published the first RPG, *Dungeons & Dragons*, in 1974. Inspired by J. R. R. Tolkien's *The Lord of the Rings* and stemming from their own interests in the popular war games released only two decades before, *Dungeons & Dragons* was a game based in a generic fantasy-world setting. Needless to say, it was an incredible success. By the 1980s, *Dungeons & Dragons* was bringing TSR profits in the millions and even had a Saturday-morning cartoon show based on it. *Dungeons & Dragons* consists of rule books that outline character classes and gameplay structure. Players create their own characters, and a gamemaster constructs a narrative that the players participate in interactively. As players improvisationally traverse through the imaginary world, they meet people with whom to speak, monsters with which to fight, and quests in which to partake. The gamemaster plays all of the non-player characters. At its very heart, an RPG is a performance in which players, like actors, assume a role and live it out through imaginary circumstances. By acting in a specific imaginary environment, players are asked to recall behavioral patterns specific to that universe. For example, a character playing the role of a smuggler in a *Star Wars*–based RPG would look to the movies to form an idea of how his or her character would act. The same is true for a game based on Tolkien's *The Lord of the Rings*; a player playing an orc will attempt to mimic the behavioral patterns of the orcs as described in Tolkien's literature. In this way, the performance created by the movie or novel is continued, and the behavior of the characters from it is (as Schechner would say) restored. The "strips of behavior" can be taken from the source of the RPG's conception, which besides a film or novel, also includes the rule book. The rule book is in fact the most important piece in shaping the players' performance, for it is from the rule book that a character sheet is created. The character sheet defines the character's abilities and handicaps, limiting or extending the behavioral possibilities for a player's character.

Ultima Online follows a similar structure, in which, at the start of the game, a player must choose the class, profession, and abilities of the character. In some RPGs, values are assigned by the rolling of dice. For example, if a player wants to figure out an ability of his character, he roles a die. Whatever number comes up is then assigned to this ability. In *Ultima Online*, a player may choose a template of a character, like a Thief which automatically puts value on "snooping," "stealing," and "lockpicking," or may assign values to any three (but only three) skills of his or her choice. The total points given are sixty-five, and these can be distributed among the three skills in any way the player chooses. As the character further develops in *Ultima Online*, the values assigned to the abilities increase to reflect the character's increase in skill (see Scott 1997: 20).

The world of *Ultima Online* is known as "Britannia," and it is entered through a graphical interface. A session of *Dungeons & Dragons* is usually played by players in person, but *Ultima Online* is set up like a Nintendo game, in which the player sees his or her character within a virtual environment on the screen. A player of *Ultima Online* has a bird's-eye viewpoint of his or her character, which allows the player to see others and the environment more efficiently. The atmosphere is composed of generic medieval/fantasy icons, including dragons, magic, and guilds. Even though the world of *Ultima* is not new, it has been incorporated in several linear, one-player computer games, starting with the popular *Ultima Underworld* in the early 1980s. Though *Ultima Online* has its own version of the English language, that too is borrowed. The character of Josephus the Scholar describes "Britannian" as a form of English "based loosely on Elizabethan English" (*http://cob.crossroadrpg.com*). Josephus has written a guide to speaking Britannian and to forming correct sentences using the pronoun and verb changes common to Elizabethan English. There is even a growing lexicon he has formed to better acquaint the visitors of Britannia with the meanings of obscure insults and compliments. Though this obvious "restoration of medieval behavior" to fit the setting is interesting, what is more fascinating is how the players have opted to create their own "restoration of behavior" from many cultural influences. There is even a clan of vampires in the game who do not have any specific skills given to them by the computer program. Despite this, players still choose to role-play them as if they were vampires, going out at night and murdering people for blood. For a while there was even a clan of cross-dressers that physically altered their graphics by wearing the opposite gender's clothing. This latter example can only be taken as a strip of behavior derived from our present-day society, since mention of cross-dressers cannot be found in the literature of Tolkien. Having seen that the possibilities are completely up to them, the players have taken the liberty to incorporate whatever their imaginations can conjure up. At the same time, it reveals players' deepest desires— desires that, in most cases, cannot be performed in everyday life.

Ultima Online can be played twenty-four hours a day, every day of the year. With five servers that can house up to ten thousand players each, not including non-player characters, it is a performance that never finishes because, technically, the last spectator-participant never leaves. New quests are constantly being generated by the gamemasters as well as by the players themselves. If it cannot end because there are too many people constantly logging on, the question arises to whether or not it is just an incredibly long performance, or a new society set in cyberspace.

Perhaps this question cannot be answered just yet, but one must consider the cultural characteristics that have worked themselves into *Ultima Online*. For one, there are "national" holidays: holidays that celebrate famous figures in the history of *Ultima* and holidays that coincide with harvest dates. On those days, certain towns throw parades and festivals. Personal holidays also occur. Birthdays and wedding anniversaries are celebrated with parties in which numerous characters gather into a room, sometimes around a table covered with virtual food, and socialize. Guilds, major components of the social structure, usually have nights when the members gather to discuss pressing issues and ideas, much like a district or town council would in the real world. Characters even go on dates. Of course, wars are fought and holy relics are found, but much of the game is played as one would play "house," in which the tasks of mundane life (going to work, making dinner, and mowing the lawn) are role-played out. "Commerce, politics, feuds, you name it, we do it," states Oron Ironfist, Guildmaster of the Veterans of Britannia. Though he agrees that *Ultima Online* is just a game, Mr. Ironfist adds that "Ultima Online deals out its own form of stress and can be as grinding as life" (1998). Many players ask for that daily grind. Some choose to become bakers or tailors or even choose to enter a life of mendicancy, begging for their livelihood. Others become merchants and advertise their wares in classified ads that can be found in virtual newspapers found on webpages. "What I find interesting is that even the mundane occurs," suggests Agony Creed, a veteran player. "People come home from a long day at work, log on, and start ... to work. The miners, merchants, and bowyers spend hours of free time, completing boring and repetitive tasks for the privilege of completing them." Other players have cited a vibrant sense of community in the game. "There are murderers and preachers," states Shatten, a mage and resident of the city of MoonGlow, "and you can stop anybody on the street and they will have an opinion on the current state of affairs in Britannia, just like in any big city." In these ways, the strips of behavior of everyday community life are restored and expanded upon.

However, despite the seemingly player-generated aspects that have made *Ultima Online* cultural, one must assume, given knowledge of Origin Systems's promotion of the game, that a virtual society is what they designed. One can use the theories of Barthes to find the codes in the language that Origin Systems utilized to promote *Ultima Online*. The first lexia or signifier in the mantra that opens this chapter is in the word "fantasy," which connotes something beyond reality and fantastic. It brings up images of dragons and knights and furry-footed hobbits. By citing "fantasy," Origin Systems is taking full advantage of the already-established wealth of history behind the fantasy genre, but by saying "It's more than a fantasy," they are suggesting that *Ultima Online* is more effective or engaging than previous, "lesser" forms of fantasy. The second lexia is at the end of the second line and is in the phrase "it never ends." This gives their product infinite worth, for they are claiming that the experience will continue forever, thus rendering all other games obsolete. They are promising infinite "fantasy" at a low price. The third and fourth lexias are "beyond life" and "more ... than you can imagine," in the third and fourth lines, respectively. They both play off a similar idea that what is being offered is something so unbelievable that you alone would never be able to experience it. By claiming that something can go "beyond life," Origin Systems is at the same time offering that everyday life is a boring premise, and that if you could go beyond it or *escape* it, then your dreams would be fulfilled. Citing that the experience is something more "than you can imagine" is at once insulting to the person and daring. It suggests that the game goes beyond the scope of the reader's imagination and eclipses whatever fantastic dreams the reader might have. The very last line is the most interesting: "Are you with us?" This line, like the others, has the focus of "you" in its structure, but the focus is directed much more sharply than before — it connotes an ultimatum or dare. It reminds the listener of situations of peer pressure when a group of kids were doing something exciting or wrong and asked you to take part in it, to take part in a *secret*. On one level this makes the person reading it feel special, but on another level it makes the reader feel pressured. Those who do not accept the invitation will not be "cool" anymore.

Origin Systems milked this idea for all it was worth in their advertisements. The advertisements during 1996 and 1997 were composed of images of a person, or rather just the outline of a person's form. The ambient lighting, shrouding the figure in more shadow than light (suggesting something more fantastic than life), was bright enough to pick up a small piece of ornate jewelry, which appeared as a necklace or an earring, but would nonetheless appear in every ad, next to the heading, "Are you with us?" The jewelry implied a secret society, one full of mystery, adventure, and treasure. Most of the people in the ads reminded one *Ultima Online* player, Steven Zaharakis, of "either gypsies or circus freaks." The odd nature of the person also suggests that if you are different in any way (which kid hasn't felt different?), then you should join. In the end, when the player purchased the special edition released in 1997, what came in it was the piece of jewelry seen advertised. Mr. Zaharakis remembers, "When I first got the game with the pin (jewelry), whenever I went out, I put the pin on my jacket or shirt collar. I don't know why I did it. I think I thought that someone would recognize it and approach me as being a part of the same group" (1998). This thought suggests that Origin Systems's manipulation of language and images through codes was premeditated with the purpose of creating a special society and/or community in *Ultima Online.*

By using codes to imply a virtual community in their distribution and promotion of the game, *Origin Systems* was in fact promoting the restoration of societal behavior by its users, thus ensuring a longevity in the game's success. If the game becomes a large "chat room" or public forum for common people to meet under the guise of fantasy, then it will never lose profitability. As one player answered in a poll, "It is a second society, for some it's even a first. *Chuckle*" (11/18/98). If players come to depend on it as an outlet for feelings, and if they only feel comfortable doing so under the pretenses of a fantasy game (as the quote suggests), then it will perpetuate itself until its players have socially outgrown it.

In the end, *Ultima Online* is one example of a specific type of program that attempts to combine community with gameplay. What the attempt has created is more of a societal role-playing game than that of an adventurous one. Because the performance does not have an end in sight, it may not be entirely described as a performance, and may, perhaps, be given a new label, one that describes it ultimately as a virtual or second society. Most RPGs have never achieved the complexity of *Ultima Online.* Veteran players plays the game three hours a day during the week, and up to six hours a day on the weekends (11/18/98). Players have divided up their real and virtual lives to accommodate both. Just because a life is played out within a computer may not mean it is not a life. People interact on the web in virtual communities every day and call it socializing, but it is no different from attending the Guildmaster's "First Hunt of the Season" celebration. Ultimately, like the Roman Empire, *Ultima Online* will fall, but in its wake may be a wealth of literature produced by scholars for it, but more importantly, histories lived by the citizens of it.

Vampire: The Masquerade— *A Countercultural Performance*

BY RACHEL WERKMAN

Final Ascension — a role-playing club at New York University — commenced a live-action role-playing game (LARP) of *Vampire: The Masquerade* at about 5:30 P.M. in a transformed room of the Loeb Student Center at NYU on October 17, 1998.* The eerie atmosphere was created through rich, black velvet, candlelight, and the soft strains of the alternative rock group Nine Inch Nails in the background. Two vividly red, long-stemmed roses were crossed into an "X" on the doors of room 410, and other roses were randomly strewn around the dark room. Black paper tablecloths hung stiffly over the edges of the tables, which were decorated with pillar-shaped red candles. Two tables, placed lengthwise at the head of the room, delineated the judging area from the playing area. Two or more judges sat on one side of the tables, looking official (one in a white lab coat), before the game began. The rest of the room was taken up almost entirely with a long, rectangular table that was big enough to seat all of the guests. This table was used both in and out of the game, sometimes as a dining area for the players and at other times as a meeting area for the characters. A podium was placed between the tables and served a double purpose as a prop both inside and outside of the game.

When the players arrived, they were already dressed for the game (with the exception of one of the officers of the club, who changed into

---

*Most of my information was gathered on that evening, but for further investigation I attended another vampire LARP on November 14, 1998, also at NYU.

her "costume" onsite). The majority of them were clothed in black from head to foot, in more formal attire than everyday wear, wearing slacks (not jeans), suits, and collared shirts. A few players were adorned with top hats, capes, and velvet jackets, and some wore street-inspired jewelry such as chains and metal-studded wristbands. Their characters, previously created by Ethan, the event's coordinator and the gamemaster, had been assigned to them well before the appointed evening and were based on the requests of the players.

Like all role-playing game characters, a vampire character is put together from a game manual, which recommends creating a character by selecting their traits in the following order: "1. Concept (Clan, Nature, and Demeanor); 2. Attributes (prioritize the three categories: Physical, Social, Mental); 3. Abilities; 4. Advantages; 5. Finishing Touches" (Rein et al. 1998:103). Each of the five steps is elaborated upon in detail in the manual, and every listed trait is accompanied by a brief description of its applications. One player explained that he had wanted a powerful, strong vampire, a "brawler," and he got one that could in fact "kick ass." This would imply that his physical attributes were the highest ranked on a scale of one to five, outweighing his social and mental traits. All of the participants describe, in varying degrees of detail, those traits and characteristics they wish to portray, and these desires are modified through the gamemaster before the LARP meets. If this authoritative presence was not implemented, players could try to bypass rules by having too many powers or skills.

Before the game officially commenced, the gamemaster stood at the podium and explained various rules and points that were specific to this night's play. He reviewed some technical aspects regarding blood pools and replenishment, and outlined the boundaries of the game in the building. Play was limited to the two reserved rooms and the hallway and the staircase in between. Shortly following this announcement, the guests were instructed to "get into character." Most of the players then pulled out their character sheets, on which were detailed their physical, social, and mental traits, as well as disciplines, status, and abilities. Also provided was each individual's clan, nature, haven, coterie, demeanor, and experience. Once this information had been sufficiently absorbed, the now-transformed players began to interact with one another as characters, introducing themselves and making small talk.

The gamemaster transformed into the Prince and called the vampires to order around the table. According to the manual, "Prince" is the title given to the vampire (male or female) who has managed to gather the most support and force. For the sake of the structure of the game, it is important that the gamemaster be at the top of the power pyramid. However, in the imaginary world this power is assailable, and the option to usurp the "throne" is therefore always available to any ambitious vampire. As the Prince, Ethan's command met with a different energy from the characters than he had encountered from the players as himself. A sense of the strong personalities, now activated, pervaded the "vampire cavern." The manual discusses the common vampirical attitude toward the Prince: "Most vampires ignore their prince, or give him half an ear at best to make sure they don't miss anything that might pertain to them" (Rein 1998:35). Indeed, as vampires the guests seemed less eager to comply with authority and took a little more time assembling themselves at the table. Next, the Prince greeted his fellow "living dead" warmly and launched into an impromptu speech about the state of the vampire world in New York City. The story picked up from the previous LARP session, in which a vampire killer had been on the loose. The Prince made a demand for the apprehension of the killer — dead or alive — and for peace between the clans. With these instructions— the threat of death to anyone who tried to leave the premises (that is, play out of bounds) and a warning not to kill one another too quickly — the meeting adjourned and the game began.

Characters who were already allied with others— as a result of the previous game, perhaps— ran off to plot together, but the majority remained sitting around the table or lurking in corners of the room. Gradually, conversations started up and characters began to "feel one another out." Almost immediately, there was conflict. One gentleman tried to convince a vampiress that he could be of assistance to her, and she kept questioning him, "What are your credentials? What are your skills?" He was repeatedly unable to answer to her satisfaction because he did not want to reveal those details. Within an hour, the judge wearing the lab coat was arranging for the forging of letters and titles, and for the procurement of magical articles. There was also a rumor of an internal clan takeover.

The playing time of a LARP is indefinite since there is no script and no outline of what actions must take place. Final Ascension scheduled seven hours for themselves, and it easily could have gone beyond the allotted time. Depending on whether or not their character survived from the previous game, players will often continue to play the same role in each session. As one participant explained, this allows the players to advance their characters to a different level. Like a television series in which the same characters face new and different dilemmas, the same vampires must deal with new friends and enemies and with different relationships and dynamics. Consequently, they will be forced to employ different strategies and tactics in every game. As in life, the outcome for each person is totally undetermined, and the risk of character death is always present.

The performance of a LARP exists solely in the moment and is based on the interaction of the ideas, perceptions, and goals of each individual player or character. These exchanges create the structure of a LARP that does not exist until that moment of collaboration among the participants. Therefore, unlike a conventional theatrical production, it is more akin to real life, retaining more of the energy of living since no one knows where the game is headed. For this reason, though the stakes are as high as life and death, the emotional commitment of the players is different from that which actors need to bring to a play. Emotional responses to the LARP's scenario arise purely out of the moment of creation; no thought is given as to where the feelings should lead or how they will or will not affect the development of the story. For example, the frustration of the woman who could not get an answer to her question, "What are your credentials?" was a direct result of her partner's refusal to cooperate. That moment conjured up emotions in her over which she had no control. In conventional theater, the emotions are rehearsed to seem real; they are manipulated for a desired effect or purpose (as given in the play). Therefore, in a play the "real life" element is merely outlined and briefly glimpsed by an audience that is outside the action.

J. L. Moreno calls conventional theater "dogmatic" in which "the creative product is given" (1983:18). He contends that the dramatist's "work, the creation of which was the very essence of certain moments bygone, returns only to deprive the present moment of any living creativity of its own. In consequence, the actors have had to give up their initiative and their spontaneity. They are merely the receptacles of a creation now past its moment of true creativity.... They have surrendered themselves to ... an extra-temporal, moment-less performance" (18). Moreno is a firm believer in producing "the moment itself" rather than presenting the moment as a product. Nothing about the LARP is player-predetermined, so it cannot be grouped with conventional theater. The aspect that becomes most important is the interaction of the characters during each moment as it is formed, rather than the telling of a particular story through a pre-scripted outline. The players of role-playing games serve their own ends and create their own realities.

As with any performance in which the specifics of its moments vary each time it is performed, a LARP is never the same game twice. However, it is not just in the details that a LARP changes. The basic fabric of the game, woven through dialogue, plot, and action, is created "in the moment" and therefore always subject to change and unable to be repeated. The content and the extent of the drama can vary depending on the game-master. At one session I attended, the gamemaster wrote out a background description of the vampire world as a reference and introduction to the evening. She gave each character a sheet of information about other characters, providing hints or clues to help initiate play. The physical pieces of paper, in this case, constituted a "written text." The speeches Ethan gave as both himself and the Prince are drama as well; they provide the "scenario." The elements of the drama that are consistent and necessary for every session are found in the game's manual, in which the rules and other written information are laid out, and in the character sheets that outline the only definitive pieces of text.

The acted script is the second stage of the drama. If the gamemaster says, "I want the killer found," the script is the development of that command in the behavior of each individual. It is the *how* of the game. All of the players in the game are, at all times, transmitting the story to one another through their interactions; that is how the story is created. How the gamemaster's scenario affects each person is how the script is "taught." As with other performance genres, in role-playing the script is not limited to dialogue. The actions each character takes that involve a judge or require approval of the gamemaster are also a transmission. This includes physical confrontations. Although the players may not really engage in physical contact, those clashes may be enacted. The outcome of such violent episodes is determined by the role of dice, or rock/paper/scissors matches, and by the addition and subtraction of points from the characters' "abilities" pool. Other actions taken by a character other than speech include casting spells, obtaining weapons, and performing rituals.

When I was present as an observer, I constituted the audience. Observers, however, are a rare phenomenon and unnecessary. A LARP is a self-contained performance, needing no other outside eyes to act as an audience. The act that each player puts on, in character, is for the other players and for themselves and comprises the theater of the event. A player may present different aspects of the character at different times to different people, therefore the performance is always shifting. In role-playing, for *each* person, the audience is formed in any number of different configurations. Depending on what trait a character is revealing or what outward appearance the player wants to present, an audience could potentially be another clan, anyone who might be within earshot of a secret conversation, the Prince, or the group as a whole. In the LARP that I attended, vampires were continually clumped in corners, whispering in an attempt to have a private discussion. While individuals are negotiating their audience, they are simultaneously providing an audience for dozens of other people. Meanwhile, groups are formed on the basis of clan, shared needs or goals, or strategical alliances. Another level of personality/character is portrayed when the players are defined as part of a group. Each person then represents a broader belief system or group objective. There is an interesting dynamic between the individual and the group in a LARP that is nonexistent in conventional theater. In traditional theater there is a sense of "us" and "them"—the actors on the stage versus the audience out beyond the footlights. In a LARP the lines are blurred and constantly shifting depending on the performance of each player.

A LARP performance is truly lived and experienced in the moment of creation in front of other people. The essence of role-playing games is an exploration of relationships. Players explore parts of themselves in relation to others. Because the focus is on "who your character is," the character of the vampire becomes an extension of the self; it is the self in an alternative lifestyle. All of the players I interviewed talked about the game as a way to explore and learn about themselves in a new set of surroundings. Brian Chin, a newcomer to *Vampire: The Masquerade*, said that for him the LARP was the physical manifestation of his internal visions. He called it a waking daydream in which he is able to create a more vivid, dramatic reality for himself. He plays an active role in his shared fantasy that exists outside of his imagination, and he lives in the collective imaginative creation that flows among people in real time and space.

The fantasy environment creates a dynamic in which real responses and interactions can take place. The make-believe world frees the participants from the social roles they play in everyday life and permits them to experiment. For example, a female vampire led a group of male vampires and possessed the most power of anyone in the clan. There was a lot of talk about how to either satiate her (agree to her demands, or do her a favor) or bypass her altogether. Her influence and presence were great and made it difficult for other clans to avoid dealing with her. The woman playing the part, Teisha Lawrence, had the most energy and motivation of all of her clan members, and the men of the group therefore accepted her leadership. Outside the game, she shared with me that she utilizes this quality to the highest degree when she plays so that others around her have no choice but to follow her lead, while in everyday life they may actually challenge it. Another example of the players' experimentation with identity is illustrated by the men who wore nail polish and/or lipstick. One player even spray-colored his hair silver. This costuming and makeup go beyond trying to create a character to playing other genders, ages, or personal images. If they dressed this way in the real world, they would most likely receive stares and/or comments. In the vampire world, men decorated in this manner are totally accepted. It is safe to behave differently from how one usually behaves because these actions take place in another world.

This kind of imaginative exploration is typically shunned or discouraged by society. John Hodgson remarks on the suppression of the imagination in his book *Improvisation* (1974): "Every one of us has a keen imagination in early childhood, but the structure of our society and relationships tends to make us feel less happy about it. Gradually, we become anxious to suppress it or hide it until finally the power is lost altogether.... We quickly associate it with the fanciful and somehow the concrete world of reality is made to seem more worthy" (22). In this way, role-playing games are a countercultural activity because the players are actively reuniting with their imaginative powers, using them to create a fantasy and affect the "concrete world of reality."

It is not only the creativity of this kind of game that challenges the larger culture, but also its subject matter. Vampires have a mysticism in today's society that contains counter-cultural themes. They are also sustained by the blood of mortal human beings, which makes them predators and a threat to our race. They are beyond death, which gives them unstoppable power. Their world, though akin to ours, is nasty and violent. All of these qualities go against the way our culture preaches the world should be. The behavior of vampires in their environment breaks many of the social rules that exist in our world. For example, in gameplay physical assault is a legitimate way to resolve disagreements in the vampire world. While very direct expressions of emotions, especially in the presence of others, are discouraged in real life, they occur frequently among vampires.

For Teisha, a love of the "dark side" brought her to *Vampire*. For her, this interest stems from an appreciation of the Gothic aesthetic. In the game, she can explore her fascination on a fantasy level. She can experience the power that comes with immortality and "eternal strength." For another participant, the romance of the vampire myth attracted him to the game. The extremes of tragedy and ecstasy keep him "awake and thinking." The stories of vampires are "thrilling stories of terror, action and romance" (Rein et al. 1998:21). In order to enact these stories, the LARP players are called on to enact parts of themselves in bold and risky ways.

The alternative world that the players create satisfies their desire to explore power within themselves and their imaginations. It may be that they function better in everyday life because they have another world in which to live. Exploring under imaginative conditions is a way to test out different behaviors and/or points of view in an environment free of real-world consequences. Ultimately, however, exploration of behaviors and relationships in an imaginary world may lead to self-understanding that can be applied in everyday life.

PART VIII

Environmental Fantasies

Participation in Another Dimension

BY ALISON VASAN

The Hollywood Tower Hotel looms gloomily at the end of Sunset Boulevard. Decaying and dark, the now-closed hotel still stands majestically, echoing of actors and actresses who slept in its rooms, producers who strolled through its gardens, and movie star wanna-bes who gazed at its gates. Looking past the lower buildings to the thirteen-story-tall tower centerpiece, one's eyes are drawn to a now-exposed elevator shaft. You watch as an elevator appears in that shaft and then, as the screaming starts, disappears. The elevator falls down the shaft, plunging all of its occupants into the gloomy depths of the basement and beyond. This Hollywood Tower Hotel is not a death trap but the stage for Disney's Twilight Zone Tower of Terror, placed at the end of their Sunset Boulevard area at Disney's MGM Studios at Walt Disney World near Orlando, Florida. The thrill of this free-fall ride, like others many at theme parks across the country, lies in the Tower of Terror's thirteen-story drop. It is the distinctive Disney touches, however, that make the ride unique. These include acceleration of the free-fall drop and use of iconography from *The Twilight Zone* television show (1959–1964) in order to form a context for the ride. By using identifiable codes from *The Twilight Zone*, Disney intended to create an environment that would make the average park visitor a participant in the fantasy.

The Tower of Terror was originally conceived for the thrill of the free-fall ride itself, but Disney has never been a company to eschew style, and as such, a story had to surround the ride. Since the ride would be at their MGM Studios, a radio-, television-, and film-themed park, the ride had

181

to reflect one of those three areas. The original idea for the surrounding story focused on the owner of the hotel murdering all of his guests during a film wrap party, but that idea did not get very far with family-oriented Disney. Another story line idea centered on a group of movie stars who disappeared while staying at the hotel. Guests would only discover that the actors had vanished into the elevator once they themselves had already been strapped in. This idea, however, was also deemed unacceptable. Disney chair and CEO Michael Eisner insisted that the riders play a part in the story, and the Imagineers—employees in the creative engineering division of Disney—came up with the idea that the riders were actors in an episode of *The Twilight Zone*.

When Imagineers set out to create a new ride, it is not the same process as when another theme park might make a new attraction. The Disney Corporation has its own aesthetic, its own look and feel. "Imagineering" itself began with a group of moviemakers from Disney's studio who were asked to work on the first theme park. It is this origin in film that leads to the inclusion of plot in many rides at the Disney theme parks. Whereas a "normal" theme park might have a simple, non-looping roller coaster, Disney's will have a ride like its Space Mountain, an indoor roller coaster (meaning it can run in rain or shine) that takes its riders into outer space, letting them ride with a sky of stars above their heads regardless of the hour. From the beginning (when the visitor enters the ride's line) to the end (the gift shop selling Space Mountain souvenirs), Disney surrounds visitors with constant reminders that they are in another world. There are photographs of far-off galaxies, and, once the visitor is inside the main wraparound line, there are simulated, humorous parodies of commercials from distant worlds. Every inch of the ride is constructed as an outer-space reality to the best of the Imagineers' abilities. As time has gone by, the thematic environments created by the Imagineers have become more elaborate and more complete. Through the manipulation of various cultural codes, Disney has been able to create a participatory environment within the confines of its theme parks.

The participatory performance of the Tower of Terror begins when the guest enters the front gates of the Hollywood Tower Hotel. On days when the park is not particularly busy, one can wander through the gardens. A more "guided" tour is provided when the line forces the guests to wait, though the delay does allow them to take in the details as they make their way past the dried-up fountain and shriveling vine-trellis on their way to the abandoned hotel lobby. Once inside the lobby, the guest observes unchecked luggage next to cobwebbed bell stands and unconsumed martinis on tables, all seemingly untouched for decades. Hotel staff members guide the guests into the library because the hotel's elevator is marked "out of order." Once the guests are crowded into the wood-paneled library, the power goes out, lightning flashes, and a television at the far end of the room turns on. The late Rod Serling, host of *The Twilight Zone*, tells the guests the story of two movie stars, a child actress and her governess, and a bellboy who were riding the elevator on a dark and stormy night. They disappeared when a bolt of lightning struck the hotel's tower. He then tells the guests that they will be using the hotel's service elevator for *their* journey into the "Twilight Zone." Proceeding through a secret panel in the library, guests walk through the service area to three "service elevators." The elevators are arranged with three rows of people, divided down the middle by an aisle, totaling about twelve riders. The lap bar is lowered, the elevator doors close, and the elevator ascends a few floors. Most of the guests believe that this is it: thirteen floors, the drop, and that's the end of the ride. The story, however, has only begun.

The elevator first stops at a floor where the ghosts of the five people who disappeared in the elevator appear to the guests. Lightning flashes, the people disappear into static, and *The Twilight Zone* theme music plays. A window at the far end of the room begins to spin toward the guests, shattering about fifteen feet away from the car. The elevator doors then close once more, and the car ascends a few more floors, at which point it breaks free of the elevator shaft and travels horizontally through images from *The Twilight Zone*: spirals, clocks, and watching eyes. At the end of the journey across the floor, the car attaches to another elevator shaft, and there is complete darkness. This is the advertised part of the ride: the car drops a few stories, comes to a complete stop, and then drops several more. Then, after a second's pause, the car is whisked to the top of the shaft; the doors separating the elevator shaft from the air far above those gardens open, and the guests can see the back of the Hollywood Tower Hotel's sign before they drop thirteen stories at a rate faster than the pull of gravity. In the 130-foot length of shaft, the car accelerates and then slows to a smooth stop. The guests are given a final farewell by Serling, who advises them to be more careful the next time they think about checking into an abandoned hotel on the "dark side of Hollywood." The car disconnects from the shaft once more and coasts through the hotel basement. After guests are unloaded, they proceed to the gift shop, where they can purchase a photograph of themselves from the top of the plunge, among other ride memorabilia.

Building on the existing mythology of *The Twilight Zone* and the fantasy world of the series, the Imagineers created a new episode. Schechner might call this new episode the drama of the ride. He defines drama as "a written text, score, scenario … [that] can be taken from place to place or time to time independent of the person or people who carry it" (1988:72). The Imagineers designed their new ride upon this drama, building the blueprints for the Tower of Terror around it. In Schechner's terms, this blueprint or plan might be called the script, the "basic code of events" (72). They then carried through with this script to the best of their technical and creative capabilities, creating an acceptable addition to the television series. Riders confirm this: Michael Sprout, a show writer, attests, "A lot of people have told me they don't remember a *Twilight Zone* episode about an elevator. And they're right. This is the 'lost episode' no one has ever seen" (Imagineers 1996:163).

This is not the only free-fall ride at an amusement park. A similar ride can be found at Six Flags Over Texas in Dallas. The Cliffhanger takes four riders up the tower of the ride, pushes them out to the coasting shaft, and then drops them. As the car reaches the end of the shaft, it skids to a stop, sloping to a horizontal finish. The car is then pulled back to the beginning, and the riders are unloaded. There is no context or story line, no elaborate structure built to mask the drop shaft. It stands unabashedly as a straight thrill. There is no environment in which one might even participate. Even in its physical appearance, the Tower of Terror bears little resemblance to the Cliffhanger. Unlike the Cliffhanger's straightforward gravitational pull, the Tower of Terror uses two motors, "twelve feet tall, seven feet wide, thirty-five feet long and weighing in at 132,000 pounds" to control its cars (Imagineers 1996:163). The engines are billed as the "world's largest ride system motors" to the few people who hear about them. They allow the two "elevators" to accelerate to a speed faster than that of free fall and then slow to a complete stop without using the skidding technique of rides like the Cliffhanger. These two motors are mounted on top of the Tower of Terror's elevator shafts. Their smooth acceleration and deceleration allow for the actual ride to take place without the riders' knowing of the mechanism by which they are thrilled. Those who do notice that lack of skidding at the ride's finish are amazed, which adds to the mystery of the Tower of Terror.

Riders may not realize that they are involved in the performance as both performers and spectators. When they enter the hotel gates, they begin their own performance of the ride; they become participants. Riders only expect the thirteen-story drop, but Disney involves them in the illusion by drawing them into the mystery of the ride. As riders expect the plunge to come immediately after entering the elevator car, the suspense of *when* the thrill is coming serves to hold their attention. The accompanying fear or lack thereof also shapes the performance. Disney has provided participatory theater with their looming hotel, new episode, and unique technological application.

While this is a participatory environment, and Disney has easily allowed the visitor to become a part of the experience, observers will not see guests on the ride behaving like something "other" in this imaginary environment. A performance of a role is expected to be something different from everyday behavior. With the Tower of Terror, which is chronologically placed in the present and which invites the riders as common people to participate, no alteration in behavior is required in order to become a participant in the ride. Disney has set up the environment so that even if a guest is wholly uninvolved in the experience, he or she is still participating. The rider is merely a visitor to the Hollywood Tower Hotel, where a horrible, unexplained (fictional) occurrence has transpired. When the rider walks through the gates and the gardens, he or she has tacitly accepted this reality. The sign on the building reads "The Hollywood Tower Hotel," and one chooses to recognize this as an acceptable alternate reality in order to experience the ride.

This is not to say that simply naming something and creating a context for it is enough to create a participatory environment. For example, the Six Flags theme park organization has a very thrilling roller coaster named "Batman" at its Magic Mountain theme park in California. The ride, a suspended, looping coaster, is surrounded by signs of the *Batman* mythology. There are Batmobiles and other signs of Gotham City, but there is no story for the ride. Bruce Wayne does not come out and tell riders that this roller coaster is their escape from the Joker. "Batman" is merely a name for the new ride, and once visitors are bolted into the giant steel contraption there is no narrative to explain one's trip through the air. It merely remains a thrill ride without much narrative participation.

Disney has used *The Twilight Zone* to provide a wider context for its ride, to give the ride a meaning and a purpose. Barthes said that in order to understand the significance of a text, one must locate "the forms, the codes which make meanings possible" (1985:84). He said these codes provide connotative meanings through association. The codes that link the events and images from the ride to the existing series are easily recognizable, even to one who was born after the show went off the air. The term *The Twilight Zone* is part of the national vocabulary, and the music from the series is a sign that something has gone strangely awry. The Twilight Zone Tower of Terror combines the terms, the music, Rod Serling, an acceptable story, and a thrill ride to create one of the more popular attractions at the MGM Studios theme park. Yet, simply using *The Twilight Zone* to mask a free-fall ride is not enough for a company with as strong an aesthetic philosophy as Disney. There has to be something more to make this ride unique and groundbreaking.

Most of these details are technical aspects, unrivaled applications of existing technology in the creation of an alternate environment. Aside from the faster-than-gravity plunge, there is the challenge of detaching the elevator car from the first shaft and then connecting it to those very important motors for the drop. There is also the short segment after boarding the elevator when the five people who disappeared laugh at the riders before disappearing into television static. While this, upon further examination, is most likely a simple projection on a scrim, the following effect involves the window, which appears as a static background object before the actors disappear. Disney's Imagineers pull a simple magician's trick, distracting the guests with another effect while switching the physical prop window for a projection, which is able to spin toward the riders and then break. Yet this simple trick is still "magic." There are many other design details, not particularly technical, that add to the depth of the environment Disney presents. It is those details, present in every piece of Imagineering, that make something created by Disney entertaining for many people even upon repeat visits because there is always something new to notice and experience.

Disney's aim, of course, is to encourage those repeat visits, to create an environment so compelling and entertaining that a visitor will feel the need to return. It is similar to creating a movie that is entertaining upon repeat viewing (or which a consumer would wish to buy on video or DVD), in that there needs to be more depth to the product than that which is initially accessible. Disney does this by creatively employing outside mythologies in its theme park, thereby appropriating depth that has already been established. Thus, the manipulation of those cultural codes, and all of the allusions that come with them in the Tweilight Zone Tower of Terror ride, provides a greater context for participation, and an entertaining performative event.

The Dudleytown Witch Project: A Personal Account

BY CHRISTOPHER KAM

One summer, perhaps three or four years ago, we were vacationing at our summer home on Cape Cod. Friends of my parents were visiting, and I, being the youngest, was dislodged from my bedroom and made to sleep on the sofa-bed in the living room. One night — it must have been two or three in the morning — something woke me up. I don't know what it was; a dream, a noise. It was one of those times that you are shaken from sleep so abruptly that you're immediately fully awake. I remember sitting up because something had startled me. As my eyes adjusted to the darkness of the room, I could see a woman, standing at the foot of the sofa bed, looking at me. In the poor light, she appeared to be dressed in an orange raincoat (at least that's how I remember her). At first I thought it was my mother, and she was about to take the dog for a walk or something. I even called out to her, "Mom," as if to question her choice to be up at three in the morning. But as I stood staring at this figure, it faded away. Who or what this was, I don't know. As I recall, that summer there had been an abundance of occurrences in the house that my sister and I had concluded to be ghostly phenomena. There were, for example, knocks and footsteps coming from the second floor when no one was up there, and a phantom smell of fish would hang in the air, but only for a few minutes. My parents, the skeptics, or perhaps the realists, shrugged these and other happenings off. They said the knocks and footsteps were probably branches hitting the roof, or an animal in the attic. As for the smell of fish, well, we lived a quarter mile from the ocean, and of course there are fish smells. So, maybe this woman I saw was really nothing, just a blur between sleep and reality. After all, our summer house was only twenty or thirty years old. Don't ghosts usually haunt much older houses?

It is this ability to accept the supernatural that has been a part of my life for a long time. And mainstream culture at the end of the twentieth century has finally caught on. It is the end of the millennium. Predictions abound about the world ending soon, and people turn to the spiritual for salvation. Occult and New Age shops flourish; Wicca and pagan beliefs have become accepted alternative religions; shows like *The X-Files* have created exciting stories about UFOs and government conspiracies; and pseudo-news programs like *Strange Universe* and *Unsolved Mysteries* have investigated stories of ghosts, aliens, and psychic phenomena. In addition, supernatural events have become news: a bleeding Virgin Mary; statues that drink milk in the Far East; a comatose girl curing diseases for thousands of Catholics; and mysterious crop circles have appeared in England and then in the United States. Are these things real? Is there something more happening here? Are there things in heaven and earth not dreamt of by our philosophers? Our greatest fear is that there is nothing for us after death, so perhaps we look to stories of ghosts and belief in angels and guardian spirits for the answers.

For me, ghosts have always been the thing, though I reluctantly admit I'm into all aspects of occult. I've been to the stores. I wear healing crystals and amulets, sometimes. I own tarot cards, runes, pendulums, and T'ai Chi coins. My library has a large number of spell books. I was even a witch, for a brief period of time. But ghosts, I've always loved ghosts. They've frightened and intrigued me for years. I love the folklore surrounding them and the way they've been woven into our history and culture. Of course, I take ghosts seriously. Stories and myths are fun, but I look to the facts. I consider myself somewhat of an amateur parapsychologist, a ghost hunter. I've read countless cases about supposed hauntings. I've studied all the theories and read works by major ghost experts like Ed and Lorraine Warren and Colin Wilson. In my search to discover if ghosts do indeed exist, I take the scientific approach. I attempt to separate the myths from the facts. I don't like to mix ghosts and spirits with religion and legend. Ghosts are a part of too many cultures and beliefs to be parceled into strict Christian or Buddhist confines, for example. Ignoring the legends and tall tales and examining the documented evidence underneath, I believe that my approach is at least somewhat scientific. It's fueled by something greater, but I try to spark my interest and beliefs with skepticism and confirmed research as I analyze what could be termed paranormal performances.

Essentially, a paranormal performance — the quest for the discovery of ghosts and hauntings — is a form of investigative performance. In this type of performance, the researcher/scientist acts as both performer and spectator. Investigative performance does not have to be limited to just ghosts. Any mystery that intrigues us enough to study it is a form of investigative performance. By looking into these mysteries that baffle us as a culture, we are able to learn and become enlightened. Currently, the realm of cultural mysteries hangs most intensely around the area of paranormal research, a category of "science" that includes hauntings, UFOs, abductions, and psychic phenomena. There are stories of ghosts and UFOs in all forms of performance: film, television, literature, and theater. Through investigation and research, it is possible to strip away the myths that surround these issues and attempt to present them in the clearest, most scientific way. Perhaps the investigation of paranormal activity is a form of cultural behavior that creates an exploratory or investigative performance from which we as a culture may benefit and learn. Schechner contends that a performance comprises the "whole constellation of events, most of them passing unnoticed, that take place in/among both performers and audience" (1988:72).

In the case of this performance, my friend Kristen and I explored the "haunted" ruins of Dudleytown, Connecticut, using it as a basis for our investigative performance. All that can be seen of this once thriving New England village are stone walls and a few foundations, yet some say that there is something else there. However it is described — a lurking nothingness, a foreboding presence — this something has created an aura of mystery and darkness around the woods surrounding this deserted village similar to the fictional film *The Blair Witch Project* (1999). For the few who know of its existence, Dudleytown is a shining example of modern hauntings. This ghost town, however, has been veiled in cloud of malediction and doom from the beginning.

As in any investigation, one must first know the facts of the case. By knowing the history and legends of Dudleytown, a mood is created to structure and present the performance in our minds. Background research about a specific paranormal event and its attendant history comprises the drama and script of an investigative performance. The drama created the mystery and suspense that made the trip all the more exciting. The actual journey to the site of the investigation would comprise the exploratory and ambulatory performance, with both of us simultaneously acting as spectators and performers in this site, which became a kind of theater where we enacted the script of the drama. We would start by getting lost, then we stumbled upon a library where we found maps and a history of

Dudleytown, and then we would explore the actual site. Thus, with all of these elements combined, the investigative/exploratory performance was created.

It was a summer afternoon in late August. Like most of summer, it was humid. But not too warm; the sky was overcast, and sporadic showers made the day dark and gloomy. I went to pick up Kristen from work, and on the long drive to Dudleytown I briefly filled her in on the history. We drove north on a road that ran through most of our area of Connecticut and up to the northwestern corner where the ruins of Dudleytown lay. We drove on and met with the occasional thunderstorm. We soon left the suburban streets of the Farmington Valley and traveled deeper into the remote areas of Connecticut. Store-lined streets gave way to vast lengths of woods and open fields. We traveled through many small towns and farmland. As we neared the mountains of northwest Connecticut, the Berkshires, the farms became fewer, the woods denser, the towns quainter. We passed many a store that would have been the perfect destination for the weekend "antiquer," but this was not us—we were ghost hunters.

The road began to wind around deeply wooded mountains and through lush green valleys. We soon saw signs for Cornwall, and our excitement grew; at least we were heading in the right direction. We drove over the river we had been driving beside, through a red covered bridge wide enough to accommodate one car. On the other side lay the village of Cornwall Bridge. The main street of this town consists of a restaurant and a defunct train station. We drove on. Up a hill, and around more valleys and deep ravines. We saw no signs for Dudleytown or for Dark Entry Road. Discouraged, we began to look for signs telling us how to get home. We drove around through more valleys, always with the dark, black mountains visible behind them. I kept thinking, somewhere in those mountains lies Dudleytown, somewhere in these hills are the beasts, creatures, and the haunted ruins of the town.

We came out of the woods and down into a valley we had not yet driven through. Houses lined the road. Civilization. At this moment the sun decided to show itself for the first time. Its presence made the lawns greener, the houses brighter, and it contrasted against the blackness of the looming mountains and the grayness of the sky. We drove through this valley until we came to a stone building that stood out. It was obviously older than most of the houses. A sign in front of this building revealed that it was the Cornwall Library. Kristen suggested we go inside and ask if they had a map.

With the sun still shining, we entered the library. It was the typical small-town library, an old building with heavy wood paneling, creaking wooden floors, shelves of used books, and the musty smell of old paper. Going up to the front desk, I asked the librarian if she had a map of the area we could look at. "Oh," she said, "you're looking for Dudleytown." Yes, we were looking for Dudleytown, but how did she know? The only reason we would be looking for a map was if we were looking for Dudleytown, she said. She went over to a shelf and took out a folder. She explained that this would have all of the information we needed, and we seated ourselves at a long table in an empty section of the library. Inside the folder were maps and clippings on Dudleytown. There were not only chapters from books I had read, but also articles from newspapers. This information comprised the drama of our performance: it was the written score or scenario that would later play in our minds as we walked through the Dudleytown ruins. While Kristen read about the town's history, I attempted to decipher the maps and to determine how to get there. These maps would become a kind of script we would end up enacting in the theater of the Dudleytown ruins. I ended up asking the librarian, who gave us directions to the site.

Excited and antsy at finally reaching our destination, we almost missed the Dark Entry Road, on which we were supposed to turn. Dark Entry Road. It wound up a mountain at the top of which was Dudleytown. It certainly would have been scarier if it had not been lined with houses, but soon the houses ended and we were surrounded by the forest. The road ended at a sign telling us that we had reached Dark Entry Preservation. On the other side of the sign was a dirt path leading into the woods. We parked the car on the side of the road and prepared for our trek. We were not dressed for the expedition. Kristen was wearing the outfit that she had worn to work, dress pants and a shirt, and I was in shorts and sandals. The sun had gone back behind the clouds, making it a lot cooler than expected, and it started to rain. We wrapped ourselves in two blankets that I had in my car. The flashlight I found under the driver's seat proved to have dead batteries, and this would limit our time to explore. It was already getting to be dusk, and we didn't want to be in the woods after dark.

We entered the woods, and when we lost sight of the car beside the road, all we could see were trees. Not to be overly dramatic, but it was completely silent — no birds or animal sounds, and we couldn't even hear the rain falling, though we felt it. Occasionally we were startled by the hooting of an owl. We ventured further and further into the woods along the path, which was so rocky at times that we would have to climb over rocks just to stay on it. As we walked on, we came across a low stone wall that ran alongside the path. It might have once marked a property line or a field, but now it was just a stone wall in the middle of the forest. We kept walking, but we hadn't yet come across buildings. At one point we came across the remains of an old wooden fence, where we both suddenly thought of horses pulling wagons and using this path when it was once a main road. I had no feeling of emptiness, but a feeling of life and history, with people going about their daily lives. Almost certainly, many men and women dressed in their colonial garb walked on this road, but few had walked on it since. It was exhilarating to be on a historical site that was not some museum attraction. As we stood there, the drama of the town's history and the Dudley Curse performed in our heads.

The village of Dudleytown was settled by four brothers: Abiel, Barzillai, Gideon, and Abijah Dudley. They came to this far corner of northwestern Connecticut from England, and it is said that they brought with them the Dudley Curse. Their family, once proud nobles, had been plagued for generations by corruption and scandal. Failed regicide, political coups, and the bringing of the plague to England by a Dudley had given the family a bad reputation. As a result, the brothers were practically forced to emigrate to the New World. Making their way to Connecticut, the Dudleys settled and farmed this land, deep in the mountainous forests of western New England. They were joined by other settlers, and soon a town was formed. It prospered further when iron deposits were discovered in a nearby village. To make room for future settlers, Dudleytown citizens were kept in business cutting down the surrounding woods. Dudleytown was thriving, but with the Dudleys came their family curse.

The curse struck first within the family. One brother went insane, and he soon became the town madman. Another brother was found cut to pieces by savage attackers. Indian attacks were common, but they seemed more frequent in and around Dudleytown. Soon the curse spread to other citizens of Dudleytown. One family, the Carters, contracted a disease that wiped them all out and did not affect any of their neighbors. Other citizens disappeared without a trace. No family was spared. Many people went mad claiming that they had been attacked by demons and savage beasts. Soon the whispered fears of the cursed town were spoken outright, so that people began to leave Dudleytown as quickly as possible. By the late nineteenth century the isolated village was deserted.

Subsequently, two attempts were made by foolish skeptics of the curse who saw an opportunity to develop the deserted farmland. One man, Patrick Brophy, fancied the idea of having a whole town to himself. Shortly after moving in with his family, his wife and sons vanished and a mysterious fire destroyed his house. He wandered into the nearby town of Cornwall raving about cloven-hoofed beasts and green spirits that were chasing him. The next attempt was in 1920, when a young couple from New York City, Dr. and Mrs. Clark, came across the deserted town while touring the backcountry of Connecticut. They saw it as the perfect place to build their vacation home, something far away from the noise and hustle of the city. By themselves, they cleared the land and built a rustic cabin. Residents of nearby towns welcomed the young couple, thinking these were the sort of people who would put an end to the stories of beasts and spirits that haunted the town.

One summer while vacationing at their cabin, Dr. Clark was called back to the city. Though Mrs. Clark was reluctant to be alone at the isolated cabin, her husband assured her that she would be safe. When Dr. Clark returned to Connecticut two days later, there was no one waiting for him at the train station. He sensed something was wrong, so instead of taking a hired ride to the cabin he took the quick way and ran through the woods. Once at the cabin, he called to his wife, but there was no answer. In fact, there was no sound of life anywhere. Then, from inside their bedroom, he heard shrill, hysterical laughter. He ran inside and found his wife huddled in the corner. She had gone insane. In the time her husband had been gone, Mrs. Clark had been seized with madness. For the rest of her life, she claimed that ghosts and weird animal-like creatures were pursuing her.

That was the end of life in Dudleytown. Since then, no one has attempted to resettle the land. Contemporary visitors find no sign of life. Dudleytown is now just ruins: stone foundations, overgrown paths, and burnt-out holes where fireplaces once stood. Even today, those who explore the ruins report strange happenings. An ill-fated television documentary crew was cursed with failing equipment and ruined film. Other visitors have come away with a forbidding feeling, as if something had watched them. A few have heard shrieks and moans echoing through the woods. Some have seen looming shapes in the daylight or orbs of light that float through the trees. Perhaps what once lurked in Dudleytown and plagued those who lived there still exists. It attracts visitors like us, anxious to have contact with the supernatural, but no one is willing to stay more than a short while (see Citro, 1998:102–109).

As we journeyed on, we passed over dried-up streambeds and puddles, where the path was built on decrepit stone foundations. Small paths veered off here and there, and we followed them. Some led to other paths and more stone walls, but most just ended in a line of trees. Returning to the main path, we soon came across stone foundations, which were the buildings of Dudleytown. Perhaps they were the same buildings where the Dudleys had lived, where countless Indian attacks had occurred, and where generations of families had ranted about mysterious creatures and evil spirits that haunted these woods. The most exciting thing we found was a large, flat stone, obviously placed at the doorway to a house. We stood on this stone and tried to imagine the house around it.

We went further down the path, past more foundations, and soon came to a clearing. Here there was an open field in the midst of the dense forest. I assumed that this had been the center of town. The path veered off in three directions here, and we chose one and soon found ourselves at a metal gate. We had reached the other end of the Dark Entry Preservation. Then we chose another path, which ran alongside the one we had first walked on, but soon it veered down into a ravine that we hadn't noticed before. We crossed more ruins and traveled alongside another stone wall. Soon the path led away from the village and we were back in the woods, where we came across a large, flat area on top of a hill. At the bottom of the hill was a small stream, and on the other side we could see the original path. In the clearing we came across the first signs of life — charred campfires, beer cans, and empty cigarette packages. I remembered my sister saying that friends of hers had camped here. Well, the reality and litter of the modern world took us out of the romanticism of a deserted town. We left a small shrine made from stones, put our initials in a tree to commemorate our visit, and then decided to leave. The hike back to the car seemed to take an unexpectedly long time. We stopped a few times at the foundations of the houses to retrieve souvenirs. At one house, I actually went into the foundation and stood in what was once a cellar, searching for something more interesting than a rock. Really, I was hoping I would feel a presence or feel something tug or push me, perhaps a restless spirit, but I felt nothing. We continued our retreat. Perhaps it was the fact that two out-of-shape heavy smokers would ever hike so much, or perhaps it was the curse, but we went crazy and started acting silly, claiming we were chased by demonic creatures. The lack of any real paranormal event, however, did not prevent the script of this ambulatory performance from being played out in our imaginations. At one point we heard a noise that sounded like a high, sustained shriek. It could have been nothing, just a bird, but at the time we let it frighten us and we doubled our pace.

We reached the road and, finally, our car. It was later than I had expected, and the forest had been darkened by the overhead branches, so we hadn't noticed that the sun had set. We made a dash for the car, with our blankets wrapped around us and souvenir stones in hand. And then it began to pour rain. We drove home, actually knowing where we were going. The experience had been exciting, and with the storm outside, we added to the scary mood by laughing hysterically, claiming the ghosts of Abijah and Abiel Dudley were chasing us. Although we had not really experienced any sort of activity that was distinctly paranormal, the intentions and the reason for the experience were, perhaps, purely for the purposes of experiencing an exploratory performance — where history becomes a performance of legend.

Bibliography

Action Figures, the Musical! *www.cc.gatech.edu/gvu/people/Phd/Noel.Rappin/ GravityWeb/actionfiguresthemusical.html*

Anonymous. *Daydream.* Shippers Pics. *www.ciudadfutura.com/expendientex/daydream.jpg* (found on the site "Shippers Pics": *www.ciudadfutura.com/expedietex/fotos3.htm*).

_____. *Wedding.* Shippers Pics. *www.ciudadfutura.com/expedientex/wedding.jpg* (found on the site "Shippers Pics": *www.ciudadfutura.com/expedientex/fotos3.htm*).

Arnold, David O. 1970. "Subculture Marginality." *The Sociology of Subcultures.* Berkely: Glendessary Press.

Ask Godzilla. *randomhouse.com/kids/godzilla/ask.html* visited on 11/19/98.

Auslan, Anita. 1998. Email interview by Heather Fitch. 28 October.

Austin, J. L. 1975 [1962]. *How to Do Things with Words.* Cambridge: Harvard University Press.

Barry's Temple of Godzilla. *stomptokyo.com/godzillatemple/*

Barthes, Roland. 1985. "Textual Analysis of a Tale of Poe." In *On Signs,* edited by Marshal Blonsky. Baltimore: John Hopkins University Press, 84–97.

_____. 1972. [1957.] *Mythologies.* Translated by Annette Lavers. New York: Hill and Wang.

Baudrillard, Jean. 1983. "What Are You Doing After the Orgy?" *Traverses* (29 October).

Blonsky, Marshall. 1996. Untitled evaluation of the future of online museology. 1–12.

_____. 1992. *American Mythologies.* New York: Oxford University Press.

Brake, Michael. 1985. *Comparative Youth Culture.* London: Routledge & Kegan Paul.

Call, T. D. "Don't Dream It, Be It: The Subculture of *The Rocky Horror Picture Show.*" *members.aol.com/maggyblu/Rocky1.htm*

Campbell, Joseph. 1990. *The Hero's Journey: The World of Joseph Campbell.* New York: Harper & Row.

_____. 1968. *Masks of God, Volume 4: Creative Mythology.* New York: Viking Press.

_____, with Bill Moyers. 1991 [1988]. *The Power of Myth.* New York: Doubleday.

Champlin, Charles. 1997. *George Lucas: The Creative Impulse: Lucasfilm's First Twenty-Five Years.* New York: Harry N. Abrams.

Citro, Joseph A. 1996. *Passing Strange.* Shelbourne, VT: Chapters Publishing.

Clute, John, and Peter Nichols, eds. 1995. *The Encyclopedia of Science Fiction*. New York: St. Martin's Griffin.

Collins, Robert G. 1977. "*Star Wars*: The Pastiche of Myth and the Yearning for a Past Future." *Journal of Popular Culture* #11:1–10.

Critical Art Ensemble. 1994. *The Electronic Disturbance*. Brooklyn: Autonomedia.

Crossroads of Britannia Site. *http://cob.crossroadsrpg.com/*

Cyberpunk 2020. 1989. Berkeley: R. Talsorian Games, Inc.

Dark Forces. 1994. LucasArts.

Dukore, Bernard F., ed. *Dramatic Theory and Criticism: From the Greeks to Grotowski*. New York, 1974.

Dyer, Rob. 1998. "Dark City" Film Review. *Dark Star Organisation*. *www.darkstarorg.demon.co.uk/fr0001.htm*.

Fannon, Sean Patrick. 1996. *The Fantasy Role-Playing Gamer's Bible*. Prima Publishing.

Fine, Gary Allen. 1983. *Shared Fantasy: Role-Playing Games as Social Worlds*. Chicago: University of Chicago Press.

Fleming, Dan. 1996. *Powerplay: Toys as Popular Culture*. New York: Manchester University Press.

Gibson, William. 1988. *Mona Lisa Overdrive*. New York: Bantam Books.

Godzilla.com. Visited on 11/19/98.

Goffman, Erving. 1959. *The Presentation of Self in Everyday Life*. New York: Anchor Books.

Gordon, Andrew. 1978. "*Star Wars*: A Myth for Our Time." *Literature/Film Quarterly* 6:314–326.

Hans, James S. 1981. *The Play of the World*. Amherst: University of Massachusetts Press.

Henderson, Mary. 1997. *Star Wars: The Magic of Myth*. New York: Bantam Books.

Hodgson, John. 1974. *Improvisation*. London: Eyre Methuen Ltd.

Imagineers. 1996. *Walt Disney Imagineering: A Behind the Dreams Look at Making the Magic Real*. New York: Hyperion.

Ironfist, Oron. 1998. Interview with Geoffrey Arend. November 18.

Jenkins, Henry. 1992. *Textual Poachers: Television Fans and Participatory Culture*. New York: Routledge.

Kadrey, Richard. 1997. *From Myst to Riven: The Creations & Inspirations*. New York: Hyperion.

Keats, John. 1993. "Ode to a Nightingale." *The Norton Anthology of English Literature*, edited by M. H. Adams. New York and London: W. W. Norton & Company, 790–792.

Keith, William H., Jr., and Nina Barton. 1997. *Official Riven, the Sequel to Myst, Hints and Solutions*. Indianapolis: Brady Publishing (MacMillan).

Killick, Jane. 1998 *Babylon 5 Season by Season*. New York: Ballantine.

Klapp, Orrin. 1969. *Collective Search for Identity*. New York: Holt Reinhart & Winston.

Konner, Melvin. 1991. *Childhood*. Boston: Little, Brown.

Lancaster, Kurt. 1998. "The Longing for Prelapsarian Fantasies in Role-Playing Games." *Foundation* #74:48–53.

_____. 1994. "Do Role-Playing Games Promote Crime, Satanism, and Suicide Among Players as Critics Claim?" *Journal of Popular Culture* #28.2:67–79.

Lee, Leonard J., III. 1988. *Action Figure News and Toy Review* (October).

Le Guin, Ursula K. 1979. *The Language of the Night.* New York: HarperCollins Publishers.

_____. 1968. *A Wizard of Earthsea.* New York: Bantam Books.

LoBrutto, Vincent. 1997. *Stanley Kubrick: A Biography.* New York: D.I. Fine Books.

Lucas, George. Interview by Rick McCallum. "Master of the Jedi." *Cinescape Insider* #4.5.

Luckhurst, Roger. 1998. "The Science-Fictionisation of Trauma: Remarks on Narratives of Alien Abduction." *Science Fiction Studies* #25.1:29–52.

Mackay, Daniel. *The Fantasy Role-Playing Game: A New Performing Art.* Jefferson, NC: McFarland, 2001.

Martin, Erik J. 1998. "King George." *Cinescape Insider* (October).

McDonnell, David. 1998. "George Pal." *www.scifistation.com.*

McKenzie, Jon. 1997. "Laurie Anderson for Dummies." *TDR: The Journal of Performance Studies* T154 (Summer):30–50.

Mergen, Bernard. 1986. *Play and Playthings.* New York: Gardner Press [Greenwood Press, 1983].

Moreno, J. L. 1983. *The Theater of Spontaneity.* Ambler, PA: Beacon House, Inc.

Murray, Janet. 1997. *Hamlet on the Holodeck: The Future of Narrative in Cyberspace.* New York: The Free Press.

Newson, John, and Elizabeth Newson. 1970. *Toys and Playthings.* New York: Pantheon Books.

Official Ultima Online Travellers Guide. *www.owo.com/guide/index.html.*

Pecora, Norma Odom. 1998. *The Business of Children's Entertainment.* New York: Guilford Press.

Piro, Sal. "Creatures of the Night." *www.Rockyhorror.com/partbegn.html.*

_____. 1997. "Official The Rocky Horror Picture Show Website!!!" *www.Rockyhorror.com/.* Edgenet Inc.

Playmates *Star Trek* Action Figure & Toys as Collectibles: *http://members.aol.com/trekshop/index.htm.*

Playmates Toys. *www.playmatestoys.com.*

Pollock, Dale. 1990. *Skywalking: The Life and Times of George Lucas.* Hollywood: Samuel French.

Priestley, Rick, and Bryan Ansell. 1990. *Realm of Chaos.* Buckinghamshire: Hazell Brooks Ltd.

Quarshie, Hugh. 1998. Interview by Scott Chernoff. "The Quarshie Quotient." *Star Wars Insider Magazine* #40.

Rademacher, Paul. *The Rocky Horror Picture Show. www.cs.wvu.edu/~paulr/rhps/rhps.html.*

Rein, Mark, et al. 1998. *Vampire: The Masquerade.* Atlanta: White Wolf Publishing.

Roach, Joseph. 1996. *Cities of the Dead.* New York: Columbia University Press.

Schechner, Richard. 1994. *Environmental Theater.* New York: Applause.

_____. 1993. *The Future of Ritual.* Routledge: New York.

_____. 1988. *Performance Theory.* New York: Routledge.

_____. 1985. *Between Theater and Anthropology.* Philadelphia: University of Pennsylvania Press.

_____, and Willa Appel. "Introduction." In *By Means of Performance: Intercultural Studies of Theatre and Ritual,* edited by Richard Schechner and Willa Appel. New York: Cambridge University Press, 1990.

Scott, Ken. 1997. *Origin's Official Guide to Ultima Online*. Houston: Prima Publishing.

Sleen, Jamie. 1998. Personal interview by Heather Fitch. 20 October.

Smith, Joshua. 1998. E-mail interview by Heather Fitch. 28 October.

Smithsonian Exhibit. "*Star Wars:* The Magic of Myth." October 1997.

Stanislavski, Konstantin. 1936. *An Actor Prepares*. Translated by Elizabeth Reynolds Hapgood. New York: Theatre Arts Books.

Star Trek Action Figure, Toy, and Science-fiction Collectibles, Featuring Playmates Page: *www.setitrek.com*.

Star Trek Playmates Action Figure Page: *www.unc.edu/~lbrooks2/ playmate.html*.

Star Warped. 1997. Parroty Interactive.

Sutton-Smith, Brian. 1986. *Toys as Culture*. New York: Gardner Press.

Tal, Katzir (prepared and edited). 1995. "*The Rocky Horror Picture Show* Movie Script." *www.geocities.com/Hollywood/4198/script.txt*.

Thompson, Ryan. 1998. E-mail interview by Heather Fitch, 28 October.

Toffler, Alvin. 1970. *Future Shock*. New York: Random House.

Tomart's Action Figure Magazine.

Tulloch, John, and Henry Jenkins. 1995. *Science-Fiction Audiences: Watching* Doctor Who *and* Star Trek. London and New York: Routledge.

Turner, Graeme. 1998. *Film as Social Practice*. New York: Routledge.

Ultima Online Strategy and Statistics. *http://uoss.stratics.com/*.

Warhammer Player's Handbook. 1990. Buckinghamshire: Hazell Brooks Ltd.

Wheatley, Margaret J., and Myron Keller-Rogers. 1969. *A Simpler Way*. San Francisco: Berrett-Koehler.

Woods, Bob. 1998. Editorial. *Star Wars Galaxy Collector*. August:2.

www.aint-it-cool-news.com. Accessed 5/17/99.

www.doc-h.demon.co.uk/shining.htm.

www.hasbro.com.

www.riven.com.

www.Rockyhorror.com.

www.Rockyhorror.com/proplist.html.

www.myst.com.

www.sirstevesguide.com.

www.starwars.com.

www.theforce.net.

X-Wing v. Tie-Fighter. 1997. LucasArts.

Young, Robert S. "Action Figures/Collectibles." Online essay. No URL.

Zaharakis, Steven. 1998. Interview with Geoffrey Arend. October 24.

Zito, Stephen. 1978. "George Lucas Goes Far Out." *American Film* (April):13.

Index